GIVE ME
A CHANCE

GIVE ME
A CHANCE

GAIL RENARD

**WALKER
BOOKS**

Opposite and previous pages: A glimpse of my
Beatlemaniac's bedroom, along with the original
camera and typewriter I used at the Bed-In.

All quotes are taken from Gail Renard's journal, as written at the time of events, or from the public domain/film clips. Events and conversations are described as recollected by the author.

First published 2010 by Walker Books Ltd
87 Vauxhall Walk, London SE11 5HJ

2 4 6 8 10 9 7 5 3 1

Text, photographs and illustrations © 2010 Gail Renard

This book has been typeset in Plantin and Trixie

Printed and bound in China

British Library Cataloguing in Publication Data:
a catalogue record for this book is available from the British Library

ISBN 978-1-4063-2307-8

www.walker.co.uk

Dedicated to John and
Yoko, with thanks.

And also to my
parents, who made
it all possible.

PREFACE

WELCOME TO 1969

1969 could be great if you were young. It was a year of optimism, hope and adventure. Most of us had long hair; many were hippies. School, street and home resonated with cries of "Get your hair cut!"

Music festivals flourished. Woodstock ("AN AQUARIAN EXPOSITION: 3 DAYS OF PEACE & MUSIC") drew 400,000 people to a dairy farm in upper New York State to listen to four days of music from Jimi Hendrix, Janis Joplin, Joan Baez and scores more.

It was a time of surprises and innovation. On television, *Monty Python's Flying Circus* and *The Benny Hill Show* started in Britain, and *Sesame Street* premièred in the USA. In *Coronation Street*, Ken Barlow was still a young man.

In education, Harold Wilson, the Prime Minister of the United Kingdom, helped to pioneer the Open University, whose courses were open to anyone regardless of qualifications and could be studied anywhere in the world.

Science also braved new frontiers. We all watched our tellies breathlessly as the American astronaut Neil Armstrong became the first man to walk on the moon: "That's one small step for man, one giant leap for mankind." The first artificial heart was implanted and Concorde, the supersonic passenger airliner, took its maiden flight.

On a bleaker note, in America there were race and civil-rights riots. The war in Vietnam still raged, at huge cost to human life, the casualties numbering in the millions. Opposition to American President Richard Nixon and the war grew as the world learned about the US's secret bombing of Cambodia and the atrocities committed against innocent civilians.

Conversely, the peace movement grew. Millions around the world attended anti-war demos and rallies; it was a time of revolution and protest. Young people found their voices as never before. As William Wordsworth wrote about the French Revolution in 1789, "Bliss was it in that dawn to be alive, But to be young was very heaven!"

Or, as John Lennon might have said, "You shoulda been there."

JOHN LENNON & YOKO ONO
PEACE BED IN MONTREAL

BY GAIL RENARD

MAY 27 TO JUNE 3, 1969

Based on my eight
days at John Lennon's
and Yoko Ono's Bed-In
for Peace in Montreal,
Canada, in 1969.

There were hundreds
of people at the
Bed-In, each with
their own story.

This is mine.

Canadian Beatles Fan Club

OFFICIAL MEMBERSHIP CARD

Name GAIL RENARD

Address 4940 PLAMONDON AVE.,

City MONTREAL   Prov. QUEBEC

No. 500,049

President _[signature]_   Jody Fine

My prized Beatles Fan Club card. I joined at the start in 1964 and there were already over half a million members.

ONE

MAGICAL MYSTERY TOUR

I was sixteen in 1969 and I'd been a Beatles fan for as long as I could remember. I was living in the frozen north of Montreal, Canada – which is fine if you're a moose.

Don't get me wrong. Montreal is a splendid place to live, especially if you like maple syrup and winter sports. If you think about it, they're an ideal combination: one makes you fat and the other makes you slim.

I adored my mother and father, who have always been kind and generous. My folks had even bought us the first colour television on the street; no loving parent could do more. And on a good day, I even liked my big brother – though not as much as I did our dog. But let's be fair: the dog had a pedigree.

I couldn't complain – mainly because I was a kid and no one would listen. There was nothing really wrong, but I was bored. I felt as if I was waiting for my life to begin, but I wasn't sure how that should happen. And suddenly the Beatles and their music came along and all the lights seemed to switch on. I swear the sun even shone a bit brighter once they were in my life.

You could follow my growth through the Beatles, even better than with one of those wallcharts where you record your height. I can remember where I was and what I was doing when I first heard every single one of their songs. I was eleven and had just finished a piano lesson when I first heard "She Loves You". It zapped through me like an electrical charge.

It was totally different from anything I'd ever heard before, especially since my brother was into bands who put the *bla* in bland, and my parents played *The Sound of Music* non-stop. The Beatles' music was young, vibrant and new. I felt that the band spoke to me, and me alone, and that they understood me. It made me feel happy, hopeful and special just to listen to them – pretty good for a three-minute song.

I wasn't the only one who felt like that. Beatlemania, as it became known, swept the world. The band had fans in every country, and my friends and I were some of the biggest. We just couldn't get enough of them, and we bought every souvenir we could get our hands on. Between us, we had Beatles books, magazines, handbags, hats, T-shirts and scarves. If they'd made Beatles underwear, I'd have worn that as well.

Then came the amazing day when it was announced the Beatles were going to be on the telly. At that point they had three songs in the Top Ten, and they were being flown to America to appear on *The Ed Sullivan Show*. Luckily we could see that show in Canada too, or I'd have emigrated. I counted the hours. I'd reserved the family's TV weeks in advance and set up camp in front of the set.

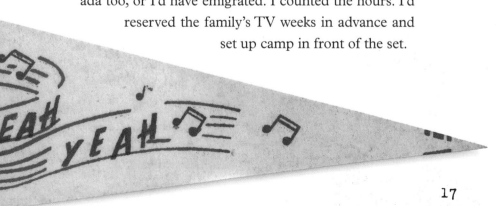

The night the Beatles were on, they played live and 73 million viewers tuned in. Make that 73 million and me. It was the biggest audience television had ever known. I envied the fans actually there in the studio, who were mainly girls about my age. They were screaming and crying, obviously having the time of their lives – near to my idols while I could only wish and dream.

I watched every second. If I'd sat any closer to the TV I'd have been inside it. As the Beatles played their new single, "I Want To Hold Your Hand", I thought I would explode with happiness. And have I mentioned they were handsome?

The Fab Four, as we fans also called them, were in their early twenties and gorgeous beyond belief: John, Paul, George and Ringo. By this point, I read everything I could about them; I had never studied that hard at school.

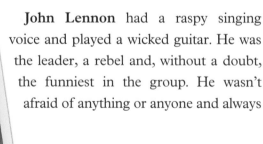

John Lennon had a raspy singing voice and played a wicked guitar. He was the leader, a rebel and, without a doubt, the funniest in the group. He wasn't afraid of anything or anyone and always

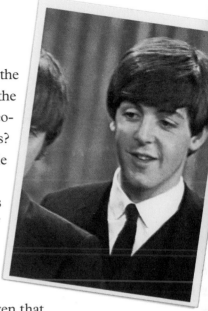

seemed to say what he thought. When the Beatles played a concert in front of the Royal Family, John said, "Will the people in the cheaper seats clap your hands? And the rest of you, if you'll just rattle your jewellery."

Paul McCartney was the bass guitarist and had the voice and face of an angel. Everyone, including mums, loved him – but we forgave Paul even that.

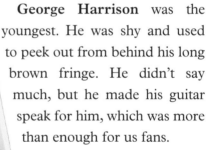

George Harrison was the youngest. He was shy and used to peek out from behind his long brown fringe. He didn't say much, but he made his guitar speak for him, which was more than enough for us fans.

Last but never least was **Ringo Starr**, the oldest and the drummer. He was known as Ringo because he wore so many rings on his fingers. It was a wonder he could lift his drumsticks.

Together, with their music, the Beatles made magic. They had over twenty Number One singles in six years. Not only that, but John, Paul and George wrote most of their own songs. Their style was forever changing and no one could ever guess what they were going to do next. But where they led, the world followed and the world loved them. And so did I.

The Beatles started many new fashions. Everyone wanted to dress like them, talk like them and wear their hair long with a fringe like them. On top of that, they all came from Liverpool, which sounded really romantic to me. My friends and I just couldn't get enough of them. They were ours.

It was a special day whenever the Beatles released a new single or album. My girlfriends and I would race down to the shops in our miniskirts and vinyl boots to buy it, then hurry home and listen to it in my bedroom. We concentrated on every note and every word, and played each track again and again. We spent a lot of time sprawled on my bed, earnestly discussing which of the Fab Four was our favourite. From the start, John was always mine. No contest.

Gazing at the latest Beatles album cover, I feared that would be the closest I'd ever get to John. My home was three thousand miles away from his. The chances of my meeting him were less than of my going to the moon.

Then one afternoon, on 27 May 1969, there was a crackly announcement on my transistor radio. The battery was low and I was only half-listening, but I heard a newsreader announce that John Lennon and his new wife, Yoko Ono, had come to Montreal. I was sure I must have heard it wrong. I had wanted it so much, my mind must be playing tricks on me. Besides, I didn't think anyone ever came to Montreal of their own free will.

Just to be sure, I raced into the sitting room and switched on the telly. And there were John and Yoko on our local news. They were dressed all in white and arriving at the Queen Elizabeth, a grand hotel in the centre of the city, only twenty minutes from where I lived. John said they were there to have a "Bed-In", whatever that was, and to talk about peace. I didn't understand what he meant, but anyway all I cared about was that they were so near. John also mentioned that he and Yoko were on their honeymoon.

I'd already done some research on John's new wife. I knew that Yoko was born in Japan and her name meant "Ocean Child". She'd written books, made films and had art shows. I could see that she was talented and original and would appeal to someone like John. It was only because of their marriage that the public was now getting to find out about her. As John himself said, "Yoko's the world's most famous unknown artist.

Everybody knows her name, but nobody knows what she does."

Before the report had finished, I knew what I was going to do. I'd finished my exams, so I didn't have any homework – not that it would have made any difference; wild horses couldn't have kept me from seeing John and Yoko. I left a note for my mum, telling her I'd be home for dinner, jumped on the 165 bus and headed straight for the Queen Elizabeth Hotel. As I got near I got caught in a traffic jam, which was agony, then ran the last part of the way, impressing even myself. I usually never moved so fast unless chocolate cake was involved.

While I ran, I also began to wonder whether I might be able to write a piece about the Lennons. The thought was electrifying.

Confession time. I'd always dreamed of being a writer, but I'd never dared tell anyone in case they laughed at me. There's nothing worse than being mocked or not taken seriously when you've confided something close to your heart. Sometimes it's easier not to say anything at all.

I'd written comedy sketches, which friends and I performed; I was also a reporter for my school newspaper – but the subject matter was less than riveting. Here was the scoop of a lifetime: the Lennons were in my town!

When I got to the hotel, I was amazed to see a huge crowd outside. It hadn't occurred to me that I might not be the only one with the same brilliant idea. After all, I wasn't the only Beatlemaniac in the world. There was a sea of fans, all pushing and shouting, begging to see the Lennons. They hadn't a hope, and were held back behind barriers by the police.

This wasn't looking good. Never mind getting close to the Lennons; right now there was no way I could even get near the hotel's entrance. But having come this far, I knew there was no way I'd turn back. I didn't know the meaning of the word "failure".

Someone in the crowd was listening to a portable radio, and shouted that the Lennons had a suite on the seventeenth floor. Along with everyone else, I screwed up my eyes and squinted upwards, but try as I might I couldn't see a thing. It was excruciating knowing that my hero was so near and yet so far; I'd never felt so frustrated in my life, not even when doing algebra.

I decided to take action. I tried to duck under a barrier, but a policeman spotted me immediately and yelled at me to get back with the others. He obviously didn't know who I was! I mustered all my dignity – which didn't take long – and told him I was a reporter and wanted to write an article for my school newspaper. Somehow he didn't seem impressed. I wondered if he'd seen our paper.

I couldn't think what else to do and was about to head for home, depressed and defeated, when I had a brainwave. I realized everyone was looking at the hotel – and no one was bothering about me. Breaking away from the crowd, I casually circled the building, curious to see what was round the back.

To my surprise, there wasn't a soul there; all the guards were in front. I could see a fire escape on the side of the hotel, which went all the way to the roof. It made me dizzy just to look up.

I've always had a fear of heights, but now wasn't the time to think about that – not when this might be the only chance I'd ever get to see John Lennon. I knew that if I thought about it too much, I wouldn't do it. I took a deep breath, said a quick prayer covering every possibility I could think of, and started to climb up the fire escape. It clanked scarily with every step I took but I tried not to look down, or up, or sideways. It didn't help. I was still petrified.

As I climbed, I hastily thought of a plan. It'd be pointless to climb all the way up to the seventeenth floor, where there would probably be security people who would just send me away. To go all that way for nothing would be unbearable. I decided to aim for the floor below, which might be less guarded, and wing it from there. As I climbed higher and higher, the muscles in my legs started to ache. I wished I hadn't bunked off P.E. so much. I counted the floors all the way up to take my mind off the pain, but they seemed to go past slower and slower.

When I finally reached the sixteenth floor, I paused to catch my breath, and looking in through a window I saw it opened onto a back staircase. As luck would have it, there wasn't a soul in sight. I silently slid the window open and clambered inside. I tried not to make a sound as I headed up the stairs. My luck was holding.

When I got to the seventeenth floor, I opened the stairway door a crack, peeked out and saw a corridor with expensive-looking carpets. I'd never been inside this hotel before and I had no real idea where I was going. But I knew I'd come to the right place when I saw a security man outside the door of room 1742. There couldn't be a lot of guests on that floor who had guards.

Now that I was here, I didn't know what to do. My plan had covered only getting this far. I watched the guard as he sipped from a container of coffee and was aware I had to be cunning. I knew I couldn't stay there undiscovered for long. Suddenly it occurred to me that the guard's coffee was very large … I crossed my fingers and hoped I might be able to rely on nature taking its course.

I was never so glad to be right. A few minutes later, the security man hurried away, presumably in search of a loo. The moment he was out of sight, I raced to room 1742 and, my heart pounding, knocked on the door. After what seemed like an eternity, it was opened by Yoko. I was stunned. I'd never imagined that one of the Lennons would answer the door.

Yoko was tiny and looked exactly as she did in her photos, only even softer and prettier. She was wearing a white trouser suit, which highlighted her lovely dark eyes and long wavy black hair. A little girl peeped out from behind her. I recognized her as Yoko's daughter from her first marriage, Kyoko. Softly, Yoko asked me what I wanted. Good question, I thought, stuttering bravely, "Could I please have an interview for my school newspaper?"

At that moment, the security man came rushing back from his loo break. Seeing me, he was furious, and apologized profusely to Mrs Lennon for letting me through. He offered to throw me out – but Yoko opened the door wider and said, "No, come in. John and I would be glad to speak to you."

For a moment I thought I hadn't heard right, but I didn't wait to be told twice. I hurried into the room after Yoko, leaving the astonished security man outside. I found myself in a sitting room, with lots of doors leading off it. I didn't have time to take much in because Kyoko wanted to show me her fluffy orange dog, which I was admiring when I heard someone come up behind me.

"Hi there," said a familiar voice. "What's your Christian name?"

I spun round. It was John Lennon, standing there smiling at me. For the first time in my life I was speechless. Eventually I blurted out, "I'm Jewish – I don't have one."

John laughed – but I felt like falling through the floor. "Sorry," I cringed, "I'm nervous."

"Relax," he said in a mock American accent, as he chewed gum. "I'm just an average Joe."

OK, even I knew John Lennon wasn't an average anything. He was a Beatle, musician, writer, composer and one of the most famous men in the world. More important than that, he was my idol. I couldn't take my eyes off him. I took snapshots of him in my mind, fearing I might not be there long and not wanting to forget a thing.

John was wearing a white linen suit and shirt, perfect for the sunny spring day. His brown eyes twinkled at me from behind his round, rimless glasses, hinting at both his humour and his intelligence. His long, light brown hair was parted in the middle and he was very slim. I'd never noticed his chipped front tooth in photos, but now it was obvious. He'd also recently grown a beard, which a lot of fans didn't like, but I didn't mind because John was behind it.

Yoko explained that I wanted an interview. John

good-naturedly replied that would be fine but he was starving and wanted to eat first. They'd been travelling all day and had ordered a meal from room service, but it hadn't arrived yet.

I dug quickly into my handbag, in which I carried everything in the universe, because you never knew when you were going to be stuck in a blizzard or need a pair of tights. I was glad when I pulled out a chocolate Hershey bar. "Would you like this?" I offered it to John shyly.

He stared at it, delighted. "Are you sure? You don't mind if I have it?"

I was surprised that a Beatle could be excited by something as simple as a chocolate bar. It had only cost ten cents. I couldn't think of anyone I'd like to give it to more.

John explained, "It makes a change. Most people who approach us want something!"

I could see that John just wanted to be treated like everyone else, which I could understand. It must be boring when people scream every time they see you, or don't treat you like a real person. I vowed to myself that I wouldn't do either. I gave him the Hershey bar, relieved that there wasn't any fluff stuck to it.

As he munched away happily, I told the Lennons that the only famous person I'd interviewed before was Patrick Macnee, who played John Steed in

Here's the Hershey-bar wrapper from the bar I gave to John.
Ten cents bought a lot of chocolate in those days.

The Avengers on TV, and that had been by letter. So I
warned them I might not be any good at it.

John was immediately interested about Patrick Macnee and wanted to know all about him. He was delighted to hear that the actor was down to earth – "I always
thought he was posh and upper-class, like you see on
the telly."

I kept wanting to pinch myself, because here I was
gossiping about my favourite TV show with John Lennon, just as if he was one of my mates. It was surre-
al. He didn't eat all the chocolate (more restrained
than I'd ever be) but handed some of it back, which I
put carefully in my pocket. I knew I would keep it for
ever ... not the chocolate, obviously, but the wrapper,
which was going straight into my diary, because John
had touched it. Then I remembered why I was here
and I didn't want to waste my golden chance to get
this scoop. I wanted to look professional, so I took out
the pen and notebook that I always carried in my bag.
Putting on my best reporter look, I asked John and Yoko
why they were in Montreal.

The Lennons explained that they hoped to have a
Bed-In, to campaign for peace. There were many wars
raging at the time, including in Vietnam and Biafra.

That was all we saw when we switched on the telly or read the newspapers. War made the world look a scary place, especially when you saw teenagers being sent into battle.

John and Yoko wanted to stop all wars. They wanted to speak to countries about settling their problems in a peaceful way, instead of automatically turning to fighting as a first resort. I was against war too, and was always excited to find people who felt the same way as me. It wasn't often that I agreed with adults, but I was with the Lennons heart and soul on this.

There were problems where I lived too. Montreal had both English- and French-speaking people, and they argued over which language should be used. Actually it was more than just arguing. The whole thing got extremely violent at times and there were bombings across the province. I found this terrifying. I couldn't understand why everyone couldn't just speak both languages, as I did, and get along together. I was eager to do anything I could to further the Lennons' cause.

Their plan was to stay in bed for eight whole days to get the attention of the world's press; John knew that anything he did caught the public's imagination straight away. They had originally wanted to hold their Bed-In in America, but John hadn't been able to get a visa, so they weren't allowed in. Next they'd thought about going to the Bahamas, but John couldn't imagine staying in bed for a week in all that heat and humidity. The Bahamas' loss was our gain.

Luckily for me Montreal is only forty-five miles from the American border, so the Lennons chose to come here instead. John decided, "If I can't go to the world, maybe, if they know where I am, the world will come to me."

And right now it was I who had come to John and Yoko, and was sitting there with my pen and paper. I was determined to do my best to write everything down properly, because I felt I must do the Lennons' peace message justice.

Just as we were about to begin, a trendily dressed man came into the room; I recognized him from all the fan magazines. John introduced me to Derek Taylor, the Beatles' press officer, who took care of the band whenever they were interviewed by the newspapers, TV or radio – a job that certainly kept him busy. He decided who should speak to the Beatles and when.

Derek was wearing a bright red jumper with fashionable Carnaby Street flared trousers, and had a smile as big as his impressive moustache. I was a bit worried he might throw me out, but he was very welcoming.

Derek and the Beatles had known each other for years, ever since they'd all started out in Liverpool around the same time. The Beatles had been unknown then, as was Derek, but he saw one of the band's early concerts and was bowled over by their music. He was

one of the first journalists to give them a rave review, after which they all became mates. As they became more famous, the Beatles gave Derek a job as soon as they could.

Although they'd only just arrived, Derek was already beavering away, setting up meetings. He told John and Yoko about a local DJ who wanted to interview them. I was surprised when, for some reason, John seemed to react very strongly against that particular man: "No, I don't want to do a show with him. I'd rather be interviewed by anyone else!"

Derek listened patiently, then asked, "So who *do* you want to do the show with?"

John thought for a moment, then looked my way, pointed at me and said, "I'd rather be interviewed by Gail!"

I was flabbergasted. What had he just said? I couldn't have heard right.

John was looking at me intensely. "Would you like to interview us on the radio?" he asked.

That's rather like asking if you'd like to win the lottery and have a year off school, with free ice-cream thrown in. Was he serious?

As if that wasn't enough, John had a word with Derek, then added, "The interview won't be until this evening, so would you mind hanging out with us for a couple of hours?"

OK, now I knew this was a dream. This sort of thing just didn't happen in the real world – and especially not to me. I'd gone for sixteen years without ever being asked to do anything like interview a Beatle. Right now I should be at home, not doing my homework or not tidying my room. That was life as I knew it. But John, Yoko and Derek were all looking at me, waiting for an answer.

I'd never done a radio show before. Then again, I'd never met the Lennons before. I guessed there was a first time for everything and it seemed to be today. But even though I was in shock, I'd been well brought up, and I knew my mum would go spare if I missed dinner without telling her. "Could I ring home, please?"

Derek laughed and handed me the phone.

I was surprised I could even remember my own number. When my mother answered, I tried to sound calm but ended up shrieking, "Is it all right if I'm home a bit late? I'm at the Queen Elizabeth Hotel, and I'm going to be on the radio with John and Yoko!"

My mother was used to me joking; this time I had to convince her I was serious. I really *was* at the hotel with the Lennons, and we were going to be on air together. When she realized I wasn't kidding, she was as pleased as I was – she knew how much I loved the Beatles. Of course she did; she'd heard me talk about nothing else for the last six years.

Mum wished me good luck, and I asked her to ring my million closest friends to tell them to listen to the radio too. I'd have given anything to see their faces, though just imagining them was pretty good too.

I hung up, wondering what would happen next. I'd never hung out with a rock star before, not even for a few minutes, let alone a few hours, so I didn't have a clue. In the teen magazines, celebrity life looked all glamour, clubbing and excitement. But I quickly found out it wasn't quite like that.

While Yoko went to put little Kyoko to bed, John switched on the telly. That was fine, although it didn't seem very show-biz to me – especially when the TV didn't work properly. John was disappointed because the colours were all fuzzy and it was impossible to get a clear picture.

Derek called the front desk, but I knew what was wrong.

"Oh, we're always having the same problem with ours," I said. "Would you like me to fix it?"

John thought we had nothing to lose, so I did what I always did at home: I smacked the TV on the side with my hand – and suddenly the picture was perfect. John laughed, "You should have been along on the Beatles' tours. The colour on the tellies was always lousy then!" He made himself comfy on the settee, wondering aloud what was on.

I remembered that one of my favourite films, the Beatles' very own *A Hard Day's Night,* was showing that evening. They'd made it five years before, but I still couldn't get enough of it. I joked that it was a pity that I wasn't home, or else I'd be watching it and I could see John on TV.

It dawned on him that he hadn't seen the film for years, and motioned for me to sit down beside him. "Then let's watch it here. I'd like to see it again."

I thought I'd died and gone to heaven to be sitting with John, watching *A Hard Day's Night.* The last time I'd seen it, I'd queued for hours in the pouring rain outside the Capital Cinema in St Catherine Street to get a

-Itold J that I was giving up a good movie to come-Hard Days Night.J wanted to see it. He liked the way that I fixed the colour tv, said that I should have been along on the Beatle tours, the colour used to bee lousy.
-left at 9:00 PM

seat. And then I had to sit next to a girl who yelled so loud I couldn't hear myself scream. This time was more comfortable, even though there wasn't any popcorn. Still, you can't have everything.

The title music started and as the Beatles sang, my heart raced. We watched the film's first scene, in which John, Paul, George and Ringo are being chased down a street in London by hysterical fans. I shared their excitement. I looked at John sitting next to me, then at John on the telly, then back again. I'd never known anything so strange in my life. As we concentrated on the film, it struck me that although it had been made in black and white, in some magical way my life had just turned to Technicolor.

Soon afterwards, a technician from the radio station arrived to set up the equipment for the broadcast. We stopped watching the film – but that was all right, because John and I both knew how it ended. Then it hit me that I was going to be on live radio with the Lennons and I wasn't prepared. I felt a bit sick. It was like going into an exam I hadn't studied for (and I knew that feeling well). I thought quickly of some questions; that wasn't too hard – there were so many things I was dying to ask, I could have been there for ever. I wrote them all down in case I got stage fright and froze on air. Whatever happened, I didn't want to let John and Yoko down after they'd shown so much faith in me.

Finally it was time for the show. John encouraged me just to be myself.

I started with something *I* wanted to know: "Do you ever go back to Liverpool, where you came from?"

He laughed. "I could never return to Liverpool with this long hair. I'd be mugged!" He added that he didn't have to go there to see his beloved Aunt Mimi any more, because after becoming successful he'd bought her a bungalow in Dorset. John had lived with his aunt and his Uncle George after his parents split up when he was young, and I could see he loved her.

He also told me that the Beatles had been given awards, MBEs, by the Queen. MBE stands for Member of the British Empire, and the Beatles' were awarded for their music and for being one of Britain's biggest exports. John gave his medal to his aunt, which was a kind thing to do. He grinned that she kept it proudly on top of her telly, for everyone to see. (Little did we know that later in 1969, John was to return his award to the Queen, in protest against Britain's involvement in the ongoing wars in Africa and Vietnam.)

Now we were rolling. I was beginning to relax, so I turned the interview to more serious subjects. After all, I knew John and Yoko were here to talk about peace. I was burning to hear what they had to say and hoped I'd be able to apply it to what was happening in Montreal. I asked what they hoped to achieve with their Bed-In.

John replied that they were doing it because "Most people want peace, not war."

The Lennons explained that they wanted people who were against war to stand up and make themselves heard all over the world. Ordinary people's voices were as important as the politicians'; even more so, if they all wanted the same thing.

"People have the power," added Yoko. "All we have to do is remind them they have the power."

John went on, "We're talking to anybody who's interested in peace, which is most people. Peace is all our responsibility, every one of us, and we can't just blame the government or the Americans or anyone else for what they did. It's all up to us."

I'd never thought of it like that before, but what John was saying made sense. He wanted us all to realize that we had the ability to stop wars as well as start them, which was inspiring.

"Everyone has to be proactive. You can do it. You can change the world ... I'm full of hope."

I understood all that – but I wondered why he and Yoko had decided to stay in bed for eight days. How did they think that would help?

John made it clear that it was to get the attention of the world's press, nothing else. They certainly weren't doing it for themselves: "I don't need publicity." He preferred to spend his time making music, or being alone with Yoko, but this was something he felt was more important. The Lennons were doing all this purely to talk about peace.

Yoko declared, "We want to use our celebrity for good."

John agreed that was all anyone could do. "Just be yourself, be accessible."

I saw that the radio engineer was making turning motions to us with his hand. I wasn't sure what he was doing but then I realized he was signalling to us to wind up the interview, because we were running out of time. It had all whizzed by so quickly.

I got in one last question. "What do you feel at the end of the day, when the rest of the world goes home?"

"Just tiredness and loneliness, my dear," John sighed.

And that was that. Our interview was over just as I was getting warmed up; I'd have been happy to talk for ever.

After we came off air, John and Yoko told me their goal was to reach as many TV and radio stations as possible. I offered to look up the addresses and phone numbers of some American and Canadian stations for them, to get them started. They both liked that idea.

Yoko smiled at me. "You're a creative woman."

I was taken aback. I wasn't used to being praised –

quite the contrary. Sometimes when you have an older brother you get used to being called many things, none of them good. I'd certainly never been called creative before – or a woman, either. Just about everyone, at home, at school and throughout the universe, treated me like a kid, and a fairly useless one at that. But Yoko spoke to me as if I were an adult, and I liked it. She made me feel as if I could make a contribution.

Even so, I was stunned when John said, "It'd be great if you could come back tomorrow with a list."

Did I hear right? People never asked me to come back a second time. Once was usually enough, and people often seemed to regret even that.

"You could help with the press and look after Kyoko," John went on.

In my stunned state, it took a moment for the penny to drop. "You mean I can come again?"

John and Yoko smiled and nodded yes.

There was nothing I wanted more; it was as if I'd won the biggest prize ever. Still, I knew I would have to ask for permission or risk being grounded for the rest of my life. You know mothers.

Mum was always asking awkward questions. Every time I went out, I felt I should fill in a form, explaining where I was going, what time I'd be back, and why I couldn't re-tile the roof or re-invent the wheel or do something sensible with my time instead.

I knew that today wouldn't be any different, so I crossed my fingers and rang home again. When I told Mum about the Lennons' invitation, she was as blown away as I was. But, as ever, she needed to know more. Something told me this questionnaire would be a long one.

My mum's a little lady, barely five feet tall in her stockinged feet, but she's also a protective Jewish mother and, trust me, you don't mess with those. She's descended down a long line of five thousand years of unstoppable Jewish mothers. The Lennons might be two of the most famous people in history, but she had never met them and I was still her little girl. If I was going to be spending much time with them, she'd need to know a whole lot more.

"Put John on the phone," she demanded.

I recognized her inquisitor's voice and was mortified. "Oh Mum, you can't!"

She answered calmly, "Oh yes I can!"

I knew she could and she would, and that I didn't have a choice. She'd never spoken to a superstar before, so I had no idea what she'd say. But I also knew my mum could handle herself in any situation and on her own terms. She made it clear that unless she was sure that I was safe and being well taken care of, I wasn't going to be allowed to go anywhere. The ball was in my court.

Me in the topsy-turvy world of John and Yoko.

Years of experience told me to surrender sooner rather than later, so I reluctantly handed the phone over to John. I tried not to cringe as Mum carefully spelt out her conditions to him. There was to be no funny business – no sex or drugs around her innocent daughter. As if that wasn't enough, Mum also said that I could help at the Bed-In during the day but I'd have to be back at home by my bedtime every night.

To my amazement, John agreed. (Not a lot of people disagreed with my mum and lived.) It dawned on me that Mum might have reminded John of his Aunt Mimi. Both were strong ladies to whom you gave the utmost respect.

By now it was getting late, and the Lennons were tired after their long day. It was time for me to go home. They didn't want me going home by bus, so Derek rang to get me a taxi. As I was leaving, I suddenly panicked. What if, with all the tight security, I couldn't get into the hotel again the next day? I explained my worries to John and said that I knew it was childish but, just in case I didn't see him again, could I please have his autograph? I had to prove to myself that I hadn't been dreaming.

John looked at me kindly and said it wasn't childish at all – but he didn't want to sign just a scrap of paper. He promised he'd find me a proper photo to sign another time, and also he'd make sure I was let back in again. As I left, John called after me, "See you tomorrow!"

Tomorrow couldn't come quickly enough.

- I told J that I could get him all the American tv network
& station addresses. J asked me to come tomorrow with addrs.
-Asked him to autograph paper for me, I said that I know that
it was childish, but I know that I'd hate myself if I didn't
get it.
* he said that he didn't want to sign a scrap of paper,
that he would find a pix, and sign it properly tomorrow.
Said he understood, wasn't childish.

TWO

EIGHT DAYS A WEEK

The next morning, I was at the Queen Elizabeth Hotel bright and early. Well, not as early as I'd have liked. I was so excited, I'd barely slept and had woken up what seemed like every minute till 5 a.m., after which I'd given up and got ready to roll. But something told me that no rock star would want to be woken up so early. It took all of my self-control to wait until the more civilized hour of nine.

When I couldn't hold out any longer, I jumped on a bus and returned to the hotel. I made my way through the mob of fans who were outside again; since word had spread, there were even more than before. It was incredible to think that I had been one of the hopefuls only yesterday. I went up to a security guard who was controlling the crowds, and informed him that John and Yoko were expecting me in their suite.

To my horror, he didn't believe me!

No matter how much I explained to the guard, it fell on deaf ears. To him, I was just another kid trying to get past security. When he told me to go home, I was close to tears. I thought I would never see John and Yoko again. Even worse, they would think I had let them down.

The security guard whom I'd sneaked past on the seventeenth floor the day before arrived for his shift. He vouched for me immediately and told his colleague that, strange as it might seem, the Lennons really had asked me to come back. The grumbling guard let me in. I'd never been so relieved in my life – and especially as this time I didn't have to use the fire escape! On our way up in the lift, the kind guard introduced himself as George Urquhart. When he laughed about the way I'd got in the day before, I knew I'd made a new friend.

George told me that one of the reasons the Lennons had hired him to be their bodyguard was that he was fluent in both French and English. Since people spoke both in Montreal, John and Yoko wanted to make sure that everyone was catered for. He was to be on duty for twelve hours every day, so I hoped I'd see a lot of him.

Before George had accepted the job, he'd asked John what he expected of him ... who should or shouldn't be let in? John had answered simply, "No drunks or druggies, but beyond that, have fun."

No sooner had we entered room 1742 than little Kyoko flew into my arms, as if we'd known each other for years. We hugged, and she excitedly pulled me inside to show me what John was doing.

The Beatle was sketching on some large pieces of white cardboard with a black magic-marker pen. I remembered that John had gone to art college and was quite an accomplished artist. (Was there anything he couldn't do?) I peeped over his shoulder to catch a glimpse of his work, asking what he was up to.

As he carried on drawing, John said he thought the walls were looking a bit bare, so he was making some artwork and signs to hang all around. He wanted to give the room some atmosphere and make it seem more like his and Yoko's.

I admired a white dove with an olive branch in its mouth which John had drawn to symbolize peace. It was simple, yet beautiful, and there was no doubting its meaning in any language.

John was also writing large signs which, with his usual humour, said "BED PEACE" and "HAIR PEACE". There was also a large "L'AMOUR ET LA PAIX", which is French for "love and peace". John made sure everyone was included.

Meanwhile, Kyoko was bursting with energy and

racing about – not surprising for a five-year-old who'd been cooped up in a hotel for a day. Yoko joined us and asked if I'd take Kyoko out to play. We agreed it would be best to do this before any press arrived and things got really busy, so Kyoko and I got ready to go.

I suggested I take her to Beaver Lake, which is in a beautiful park on Mount Royal, not far from downtown Montreal. There she could run and play as much as she wanted – though somehow I doubted even that would wear her out! I knew she would love it. As John looked out of the window at the glorious spring day, he wished that he and Yoko could come too. The more the merrier, as far as I was concerned. "Why not join us?" I asked eagerly.

John shook his head sadly. "We'd be besieged by fans before we'd gone two steps. It's one of the prices you pay for fame."

Till then, I'd never thought about the downside of being famous. Suddenly I understood why the Lennons had to hire a bodyguard, and realized that they couldn't just slip out to a park any time they wanted. Everything had to be carefully planned so they were protected from mobs and from paparazzi. In the past I had always assumed being a celebrity was a win/win situation. I was beginning to think again.

Before Kyoko and I left, I gave Derek Taylor the list I'd made of American and Canadian TV and radio stations. He was pleased and thanked me, saying he'd get onto them right away. I felt proud: I'd sat up until late into the night getting all the facts. I had never put that much effort into any school project, but here, I could envision the end result.

As Kyoko and I were heading out of the door, Derek gave me twenty dollars to use for expenses, such as taxis and any food we wanted. What a fortune! That would have been my pocket money for an entire month. I was determined to use it to help make sure Kyoko had a good time.

It's easy to get to Mount Royal; Montreal is built right around this mountain (in fact, it's thought to be named after it), and no matter where you go in the city, you can just look up and see it. It would be hard to get lost in a city where a mountain is always staring you in the face. But I thought the climb might be exhausting for the little girl; I didn't want her to be too tired to play by the time we got there. So I decided to put some of the expenses to good use, and we took a taxi.

Mount Royal isn't high, but when we got there we felt as if we were on top of the world. We could see all of the city around us, and I pointed out the hotel to Kyoko. She observed that we couldn't see Mummy or John – that would have been asking a lot! The air was clean and fresh, and everything was green as far as the eye could see. Kyoko was able to run as fast and far as she liked, as free as a bird, while I watched her.

She was a beautiful child. She had Yoko's dark brown eyes and shiny black hair, only Kyoko's was straight and cut in a long bob. She was Yoko's daughter from her first marriage, to Anthony Cox, a film producer and artist. But I could see how happy Kyoko was when she was with John and Yoko. She was a much-loved little girl and I quickly became fond of her too.

It wasn't long before Kyoko spotted a horse and carriage which tourists could hire. Of course Kyoko wanted a ride and, thanks to Derek, money was no object. Kyoko and I very grandly hailed a carriage, and the driver helped us in. We felt like royalty as the horse majestically clip-clopped its way leisurely around the mountain. To complete the perfect morning, we indulged in chocolate milkshakes and chips.

After a time I could see Kyoko was getting tired, so we made our way back to the hotel. But as we reached the seventeenth floor, we could see a queue forming all the way down the corridor. People had started coming to the Bed-In in droves. George, the bodyguard, already had his hands full, but when people in the queue started recognizing Kyoko and wanted to talk to her, he made sure we got quickly into the suite. I was glad when we were safely inside ... but it turned out to be even more crowded than the corridor.

The sitting room was crammed with people, all waiting eagerly to speak with John and Yoko. There

Part of the chaos that always surrounded the Bed-In. Derek Taylor is the stylish man in red on the left.

were journalists from around the world, talking to one another in languages I couldn't even identify. I watched as Derek tried to turn chaos into order, giving everyone an exact time when they could interview the Lennons. Derek was brilliant at organization and keeping things moving. He told me the secret was that he had six children, so was used to maintaining order.

The bedroom was even more packed with press, as well as TV, film and radio crews, with all their camera and sound equipment, everyone jostling for the best positions. John and Yoko were sitting up in their big double bed, in front of a huge picture window, with glorious views of the city. John's signs and drawings looked great on the walls; people were photographing them, too. There was so little room to move, even Kyoko had trouble squeezing in.

John looked comfy in bed, wearing white silk pyjamas, while Yoko wore a long white nightdress with frills on her cuffs and neck. I admired the Lennons' calmness at dealing with the press; they didn't seem rattled by the fuss at all. They were always polite and did their best to answer everyone's questions. Even though they were asked the same ones a thousand times, they always made each time seem like the first. I guessed that, being a Beatle, John was used to it – as was Yoko from her public art exhibitions. I also noticed that they always made sure their peace message was heard.

I thought this would be a good time to get some more material for my own article for the school newspaper, so I perched nearby to listen. I'd also brought along my trusty Brownie camera, which I'd been given for my birthday. As I was about to take some snaps, a photographer asked if I'd like him to take some pictures of me with John and Yoko. My mouth fell open. I'd love it! John and Yoko laughed as they scrunched over to one side on the bed to make room for me, saying, "Come on!"

I pointed out to John and Yoko that they had just got married, and I'd never shared anyone's honeymoon before. But that didn't stop me from joining them. As I sat on the side of their bed, it struck me how relaxed

John and Yoko are talking to the press. And those flowers behind them were only a selection of those in the suite. It was Flower Power everywhere!

53

I'd become with them. Just a couple of days before, I'd been a Beatles fan, listening to their records and staring longingly at their posters in my bedroom. Never could I have imagined I'd be sitting on a bed with any of my heroes, urging, "Budge up!"

We posed for photos and the photographer snapped away. I thought I'd never stop smiling. I couldn't wait to see the pictures and show my friends – but I soon realized I'd taken up enough time. It was important for us to listen to the Lennons speak, which was why we were there.

John began, "Everyone who wants to fight should go to a desert, form their own club and kill each other... All I want is for me and my friends to be left in peace." He seemed to know that was a bit light-hearted and added, "Peace should start with house-wives, with women and mothers, teaching their kids not to fight." That made a lot of sense to me. Women are powerful, as I knew from my own mother. He laughed, "Maybe then they'll see that long-haired weirdos aren't so bad."

I asked, "What do the other Beatles think about peace?" The band had been together a long time, since they were fifteen. Up till now, the Beatles had always done everything together – writing songs, making records and touring. Why didn't Paul, George and Ringo join him in the Bed-In?

I certainly made myself comfy with John and Yoko.
At least I didn't climb into bed with them!

John explained that George couldn't do what he did because "he's not as big a show-off as me". But George was definitely an active pacifist. John stressed the important thing was that we all had "to do our own thing for peace". Anyone could see that he was really fond of George.

Then John turned his thoughts to the others. "Paul is an intellectual pacifist ... he talks about it." He often spoke to them about his concerns over the Vietnam War. "And Ringo," John smiled, "lives peace."

But the main thing, John assured us, was that all the Beatles cared about putting an end to war. Unfortunately, he pointed out, not everyone felt the same way they did. There were fanatical people out there who didn't like what he was doing, and they could be scary. I didn't like the sound of that.

John became even more serious for a moment. "It's a possibility that one of us will be assassinated for peace." I shivered and refused even to think about that, but John went on. "I don't want to be a martyr." He thought for a moment, then added, "All I want from life is to be with Yoko."

I could see how much he meant it. He and Yoko loved each other, and they respected each other too. They always wanted to know what the other thought, felt and said. I envied that closeness and hoped that one day I would find it with someone myself. John summed it up: "We only ask to be together and, when we die, for our souls to be together."

On a lighter note, John joked that they had both married foreigners. Yoko added that the old barriers of borders and boundaries were being torn down. I realized she was right and the Lennons themselves had proved it. John was from Liverpool and Yoko from Tokyo, but somehow they had found each other. Yoko hoped that in the future people would live in a "global village". If we all felt that deep down we were the same, there'd be fewer wars.

As the Lennons were working so hard, giving interviews all the time, Derek made sure that there were plenty of chances for them to eat and rest. Those were my favourite times. Without all the press around, there was an opportunity for me to get to know the Lennons and Derek a bit better.

I suddenly remembered that my exam results were coming out that day. I plucked up the courage and, during one of the lulls, rang my mum at home. I could hear her ripping open the envelope – and then a long silence. This didn't sound good. But when Mum happily told me how well I'd done, I screamed.

Derek and John came running, wanting to know what was wrong – then congratulated me on my grades. I was proud, but at that moment I felt a long way from school. It suddenly didn't feel that important, not compared with real life. I wasn't sure what all that school-work had to do with my wanting to be a writer whereas, right then, I was in the best possible place.

John had written not only over a hundred songs with Paul McCartney, but also, on his own, two books, *In His Own Write* and *A Spaniard in the Works.* Both had shot to the top of the bestseller lists. John had even done his own drawings for them. I envied John all that creative freedom; being able to write what you wanted seemed like heaven to me. I asked, "What's it like to put out books, songs and films, any time you like?"

John surprised me with his answer. "It's hard to sell any films made by me and Yoko. And two of my books were turned down. Not all Beatles things are marketable."

What? I couldn't believe it. Who in their right mind would turn down work by John Lennon? My heart sank. If one of the most famous and talented people in the world had trouble selling his work, then what hope would I have of being a writer? Just as well I'd done all right in my exams.

The break was over all too quickly and the journal-ists came back in. They stayed late, until John and Yoko were too tired to talk. When I left for home that night, I heard Kyoko tell John, "It's great living with a star – you never get bored."

THREE

HERE, THERE AND EVERYWHERE

Next morning, the hotel was besieged. It looked as though the Bed-In was getting to be a victim of its own success. Just as John and Yoko had hoped, word of it had spread all round the globe. Everybody was dying to take part, which I could understand. Hundreds of people came, in never-ending waves, all for different reasons.

There were people who genuinely wanted to talk about peace, and see what they could do to help the process of attaining it. There were others who just wanted to hang out and have fun, who thought this must be the greatest party of all time. Still others just used this as an excuse to meet a Beatle. Even I could see, as I entered the suite, it was all getting a bit out of hand.

The press were squeezed into the waiting room like claustrophobic sardines. And wherever people weren't sitting on chairs or tables, they were perched on the floor, which made walking across the room like tackling an obstacle course.

There were also forests of flowers all over the place. Montreal florists must have blessed the Lennons for this bonanza. Fans and admirers were sending huge bouquets; their sweet scents overpowered the room. Less welcome were the cigarette fumes filling the air as smokers puffed away.

And then there were the gifts. Many who came to see John and Yoko brought presents; there were enough toys, dolls and children's books for Kyoko to open a small toy shop. Others brought mountains of Beatles albums and photos, hoping that John would sign them. There was rubbish and mess everywhere – it was almost worse than my bedroom at home.

A woman reporter drew me to one side and tried to slip me money. Surprised, I asked her what it was for. She whispered that she'd like me to get John to listen to her son's demo tapes, and handed them over. I told her indignantly that I didn't take bribes and that wasn't why I was there, but, if she liked, she could ask John herself – though goodness knows when he would find the time.

To make the chaos complete, the phones rang non-stop till my head ached. No sooner did I answer one and then put it down than it would ring again. And it was difficult in any case to hear callers through the hub-bub. All this traffic meant that the hotel's phone lines were being flooded and their telephone operators could barely cope. Other guests were having trouble making and receiving their own calls, and were getting annoyed.

Some of the people who rang were from radio stations, hoping to do live interviews with the Lennons. Many others were "ordinary" fans who wanted to chat to John – and I felt for them, but there just weren't enough hours in the day for John and Yoko to talk to everyone.

Derek couldn't handle all the phones, not even with the help of volunteers. As we struggled to answer the calls, he told me that John and Yoko had been doing interviews almost since the moment they'd woken up and were exhausted. Then our conversation was drowned out by singing from the Hare Krishna followers who had arrived.

These gentle people adhere to a form of Hindu-ism, and want everyone to achieve true unity and peace in the world. Their manner is kind and friendly, so no wonder John and Yoko always wanted them to be made welcome. The women wore traditional Indian saris, and the men were dressed like monks in saffron-yellow robes. They'd brought along their drums, flutes and tambourines – just in case the room wasn't noisy enough. They played their songs in the waiting room, while chanting loudly, "Hare Krishna Hare Krishna, Krishna Krishna Hare Hare, Hare Rama Hare Rama, Rama Rama Hare Hare…"

It was like being in a competition to see how many people could squeeze into a room. I could barely hear the phone callers and kept having to ask them to speak up. One person I spoke to claimed he was Paul McCartney! He demanded to be put through to John at once – but he sounded awfully American to me. I replied cheerfully, "Sure, Paul! But what happened to your Liverpool accent?"

"Blast!" he said and hung up.

It wasn't long before I took another call, this time from "Ringo", with an accent that had never been within a thousand miles of the Mersey. He wanted to speak to John. I asked "Ringo" where he was calling from. "London," he said.

Fortunately, Derek had told me earlier where Ringo was holidaying. "That's too bad," I told the caller. "You're supposed to be in the Bahamas."

"Blast!" said the man as he slammed the phone down again. I had to give him an "A" for effort.

We were running out of Beatles when almost immediately the phone rang again. I was beginning to enjoy this; I knew I could keep up the game as long as this guy could. The caller said politely, "It's George; can I please speak to John?"

I thought this was the man's weakest attempt yet, so I told him, "Oh, pull the other one."

Of course, it really *was* George Harrison. I ran to tell John as quickly as possible!

While all this mayhem was happening, more and more people kept arriving. Where from, I wondered? Was there anyone left in Montreal? In the world? Derek came across a letter left by two fans who had travelled 650 miles from Cleveland the day before to see the Lennons, but hadn't been able to get into the hotel. They'd had to return home. Derek wrote a letter of apology and asked me to get John and Yoko to sign it, which they did. But there just wasn't enough of the Lennons to go round.

John and Yoko were pros, and tried to share their peace message with everyone and anyone who wanted to talk to them. Their campaign was very important to them – but they weren't getting a moment between reporters to catch their breath. It grew more and more stressful. Camera crews were crowded around the Lennons' bed, filming constantly with their hot lights, which was clearly both tiring and sweltering. The cameras and microphones were never off them. Not only that, but John and Yoko hadn't been able to have even a short break and were really hungry. Derek ordered them some food from room service, but we had no idea how and when they were going to eat it.

It turned out Derek wasn't the only person ringing downstairs for food. The hotel informed him that people were anonymously ordering whatever they liked and sticking it on the Lennons' bill. We didn't know who was enjoying the steaks, lobsters and fine wines, but it certainly wasn't us!

I was cross because people were abusing the Lennons' kindness and hospitality. The fact that they were rich was no excuse for people taking advantage of them, especially when they were trying to do such unselfish work. I remembered what John had said about people always wanting things from them.

On top of all that, a lot of this food and drink was being spilt, staining the Queen Elizabeth's expensive carpets and damaging the furniture. Litter was piling up everywhere, and even the hotel's hard-working cleaners couldn't keep up. The suite was getting to be a pit. Kyoko had finally had enough and burst into tears. As I cuddled her, I couldn't blame her; I was near to tears myself. Did celebrities ever get used to this pressure?

As Derek made his way through the muddle, he signalled for me to come and have a word. It was so overcrowded, the only room where we could get any privacy was the bathroom – an unusual place to meet. We perched on the sink and bathtub, as Derek tried to figure out a solution.

Suddenly John stormed into the bathroom to join us. He was angry. "There are too many people in the bedroom, Derek!" He had had enough. There was so much going on in the bedroom. "I don't know what day it is any more!" He asked Derek if he could do something as quickly as possible.

We could see John meant it. It was funny to think that just a few short days ago, he and Yoko had been worried whether anyone would even come to their Bed-In; now they were overwhelmed.

John and Derek also had safety concerns. There were so many people jammed into such a small space, they were afraid someone might get hurt, which would have been unthinkable. Not only that, but the hotel's other guests weren't thrilled by the hubbub at this usually dignified, prestigious hotel. Derek hurried to see if he could find the hotel manager, to sort out some extra rooms, hoping that more space would make the Bed-In seem less of a pressure cooker.

As John and I headed out of the bathroom, Kyoko raced over, all smiles again. I was relieved she seemed happier – until she opened her hands and showed us a gift a fan had given her: a live white mouse. Urgh! That was all we needed. John was as thrilled about it as I was. Backing away, he gently told Kyoko, "I like it only at a distance!"

I wondered what we could do about it, before

Kyoko got too attached. She decided to call the mouse Baby – not a good sign. She put it down on the floor to play with and it scampered away. A moment later, with exquisite timing, the hotel manager arrived to speak to Derek; his eyes almost popped out of his head as he spotted the mouse.

The manager drew himself up to his full height and explained, with great dignity, that the Queen Elizabeth was one of the finest hotels in the world. It wouldn't do his reputation any good to have mice running around his rooms (I myself thought it would make a unique selling point). He made it clear that either the mouse would have to check out of his hotel or we would. John and I agreed to relocate Baby.

We took Kyoko and the pet back into the waiting room to see if she could point out the generous fan who had given it to her. He'd gone. I would have gone too, if I'd just been able to offload a mouse. A young Hare Krishna man kindly offered to take Baby and promised Kyoko he'd give it a good home. At first Kyoko wasn't sure she wanted to part with her new pet, but John consoled her, saying, "We're giving the mouse to the Church, to Hare Krishna and to God."

As John and I headed back into the press room, he sighed, "We're all doing our own thing for peace."

"I know," I agreed. "Mine, at the moment, is pest control!"

FOUR

WITH A LITTLE HELP
FROM MY FRIENDS

Early next morning when I arrived at room 1742, I heard Derek on the phone making an appointment for Tommy Smothers. My heart stopped. Surely there couldn't be two Tommy Smotherses? It wasn't exactly a name you heard every day. I jumped on Derek the moment he came off the phone and asked if this Tommy Smothers was The One. And by that I meant the famous one. Derek smiled and nodded. The Bed-In just kept getting better and better.

Tommy was only my favourite American comedian of all time. He and his brother, Dickie, were a duo calling themselves the Smothers Brothers. They had their own TV *Comedy Hour*, which I watched zealously every Sunday evening at nine, along with millions of others.

I even took the phone off the hook when they were on so I wouldn't miss a word.

Not only did the brothers write a lot of their own comedy material, but they were also musicians, playing guitar and double bass, and they sang and wrote their own songs too. I was in awe of such multi-talented people. And now Tommy was coming to the Bed-In. It was as though I was checking off a list of my Top Ten favourite people in the world. I followed Derek around, firing off a million questions. "When's Tommy coming? How long's he staying? Can I talk to him about comedy?"

The Smothers were intelligent and original, and made people not only laugh but think too. They weren't afraid to tackle any subject, no matter how serious; nothing was off limits. Tommy and Dickie satirized politics, racism and war – and even made jokes about the American President, Richard Nixon, which people didn't do much in those days. Their TV show told the truth and influenced a lot of people; it was their way of trying to change the world, only with humour. As John had told me, we all had to do our own thing for peace. The Smothers Brothers were doing theirs, and I was learning how to do mine.

But I was excited for another reason. I wasn't the only one who worshipped Tommy Smothers; my best friend in the whole world, Susy, had been in love with him for years. But since Tommy lived in California and

Susy in Montreal, she'd never imagined she would meet him. I seized the phone to give her the mind-blowing news that Tommy was coming. I was sure I could smuggle her into the hotel to see him.

But when I got Susy on the phone, she sounded really weird, as if she had the most terrible cold in the universe, with hay fever on top of that. I could barely make out what she was saying as she spluttered that she had just come back from hospital, after surgery on her sinuses. Her face, she told me, was bruised and swollen, and just to finish her new look she had two black eyes as well. It wasn't exactly high fashion.

Even worse, Susy had been ordered to stay in bed for a week and her mother wouldn't let her out. Susy was beside herself. Her one chance to meet her heart-throb and this had to happen! She was going to miss him when he was in Montreal, right on her own doorstep. How unfair was that?

Frantically she started plotting to sneak out and, as a good friend, I colluded. After all, I seemed to be an expert at getting in and out of tight places. But Susy's mother overheard us planning her escape and put a stop to the whole thing. She wasn't letting Susy go anywhere; from now on, her mum would be standing guard.

I tried to calm Susy, but I knew nothing I could say would help. How could she be happy about missing her life's dream? I felt even worse because I myself was

living mine. I promised her I'd take lots of photos of Tommy and get his autograph for her; it was the best a friend could do. I was now celebrity-hunting for two.

I'd just hung up when Tommy walked in. I tried not to gawp at him but failed miserably; I couldn't take my eyes off him. He looked exactly as he did on the telly: tall and blond, with twinkling blue eyes. No, I take that back – he looked even better, because he was standing right there in front of me. As Derek introduced us, I shook Tommy's hand, and had to remind myself to let go.

Derek asked me to take Tommy in to see John and Yoko. I would have rather kept him all to myself, but of course I knew that wasn't going to happen. While showing him in, I asked him how long he was staying. When he said a few days, I was relieved; that would give me plenty of time to get souvenirs for Susy.

John and Yoko were glad to see Tommy, as were all the reporters and photographers. His arrival meant that

Comedian Tommy Smothers with John, giving interviews for peace. The strange gun-like object being held in front of them is a microphone!

the press would be able to get some new photos and material for their pieces, which would help to keep the Bed-In alive in the public eye. That was why John and Yoko were so eager to have visits from lots of celebrities; as far as the Lennons were concerned, the world couldn't hear enough about their Bed-In. They knew what they were doing.

Tommy spoke about peace powerfully. He was against war and said so on every possible occasion. Then, after he had finished giving interviews, he confided that he wanted to speak to John privately for some advice. I was touched that Tommy didn't mind my staying to listen too.

John and Tommy Smothers being interviewed.
You can also see the "All You Need Is Love"
bedspread a fan made for the Lennons, complete
with YELLOW SUBMARINE characters. It's now on
display in the Liverpool Museum.

To my horror, he said that *The Smothers Brothers Comedy Hour* was being taken off the air! Their TV network was under pressure from the powers that be, who didn't like the brothers making controversial jokes about the American President and the war. They were trying to censor them. But as Tommy put it, "The only valid censorship of ideas is the right of people not to listen."

Tommy and Dickie believed in freedom of speech and expression, and thought the public should be able to hear both sides of a story, so they could make up their own minds. The brothers wanted to keep on doing what they did on their show.

Both Tommy and I were surprised by John's reaction: he totally disagreed with Tommy's all-or-nothing point of view. He thought Tommy should ease up for a bit, to save his show. John explained logically, "You can't be a spokesman without any spokes."

It was important to the brothers' cause that they be seen and heard by as many people as possible. John went on, "Get on TV any way you can and stop splitting hairs."

I don't think Tommy expected that answer. I certainly didn't. He thought for a moment, then said sulkily, "I hate long-haired people." We all laughed and Tommy added, "It's really a drag to be losing your hair when all the groovy people are hairy."

Though he was joking, I knew he'd taken John's

words to heart and would think about them seriously. After all, John was the master of getting messages
across. He told Tommy that no matter what, he should
keep at it and make the people who were pro-war
laugh. "They don't know how to handle non-violence
and humour."

Tommy managed to have the last word: "When you
don't know what you're talking about, it's hard to know
when you're finished!"

Soon afterwards, we all took a break for a meal. As
I was finding out, Tommy was even funnier in real life
than he was on TV, if that were possible. The Lennons
were vegetarians, but Tommy claimed, "Red meat is not
bad for you. Now blue-green meat, that's bad for you!"

Tommy also told us that he'd managed to give up
smoking by taking a cigarette and saying, "I don't need
this. This is harmful. It's poison."

I asked Tommy if it had worked and he said yes, only
now he followed buses to inhale the fumes. We laughed
until we hurt. I knew then that I wanted to become a
writer. What better job than making people laugh?

At one point, I was finally able to have a private
word with Tommy and I told him all about my friend
Susy. "She's your biggest fan, except for me, but she's
had an operation and can't be here today. She feels terrible. It's killing her!"

Tommy listened sympathetically. "What can I do?"

I knew Susy would like him to elope with her on a white horse, but I also knew that wasn't going to happen. I decided to try for something possible: "Could you please sign an autograph for her?"

Tommy said gladly, and that he'd go one better; he sat down and wrote Susy a "get well" note on the hotel stationery. I then asked Tommy if he'd mind having his photo taken with me. He put his arm around me and hugged me as Derek snapped away – but suddenly I worried that when Susy saw it, she might burst her stitches! She'd been through enough already. So I took some photos of Tommy by himself, just in case. After all, I still wanted to be best friends with Susy when the Bed-In was over.

Me, with the funniest man in the world, Tommy Smothers.

I was just getting used to being around Tommy when another celebrity arrived: the singer Petula Clark. The petite blonde pop star had had many Top Ten hits, including "Downtown", which had sold millions of copies – including the one I'd bought. She was here to do her bit for peace, but she was also upset and wanted to speak to John about a problem. It was funny how everyone was drawn to him. Petula said she had never met John before but was attracted by his kindness.

I was just amazed that so many celebrities seemed to have problems. Petula was rich, famous and attractive and I thought that was about as good as it got. What more could anyone want? But I was fast learning that life wasn't like that.

Petula needed advice about a concert she'd given in Montreal, which hadn't gone as well as she'd hoped it would. John told her to forget it and move on, and Petula decided to do just that – especially since so much more was happening all around her.

A steady stream of celebrities kept arriving. I couldn't believe my luck when we were joined by the brilliant black comedian Dick Gregory. He was active in the civil-rights movement, which was potentially dangerous as those who were against its beliefs often turned violent, and many good people were murdered. I admired his commitment.

Dick had even run – unsuccessfully – for President of the United States the year before, as a candidate for the Freedom and Peace Party. He joked that if elected he would "paint the White House black". He lost, but along the way he drew people's attention to important issues such as racism and bigotry. Like the Smothers Brothers, Dick used his comedy to try to make the world a better

Kyoko taking a break with Petula Clark. You can see there was never much room to move around.

place. He wanted to hold up a mirror to society, to get people thinking. Or, as he said, "I never learned hate at home, or shame. I had to go to school for that."

I was having the time of my life, but I also had the sense to know I was surrounded by courageous, special people who stood up for what they believed in. Each hour I felt more and more privileged to be there. I mentioned to Derek how incredibly helpful everyone was – but he was reading something that had just arrived, and frowning, which wasn't like him. I asked if anything was wrong.

Derek showed me a badly typed letter, with lots of mistakes. It called John and Yoko horrendous names and threatened the Lennons, saying they should get out of Montreal or else.

I shivered as I read it and quickly handed it back; I had never seen anything so full of hatred. Derek asked me what I thought and I said that the writer was a terrible typist. I asked if John had seen it.

Derek had shown the letter to the Beatle, who had only laughed – which I didn't understand. Derek explained that John, like a lot of stars, sometimes got vile letters from people. The Beatles had actually received death threats in the past. I was horrified, but Derek promised that he always showed any serious ones to the police. After that, he shrugged, all you could do was be careful and get on with your life.

I didn't think I could ever do that. I would be too upset and would be looking over my shoulder all the time. I didn't fancy living like that. I was seeing a lot of the downside of being a star. Derek reminded me that there were millions more great people in the world than nasty ones, which more than evened things out. But I thought even one menace was too many.

It was that day that Kyoko came to us and complained that she felt ill; her throat hurt and she had trouble swallowing. When I touched her forehead, I could feel she was hot and feverish. We told Yoko, who immediately called the hotel doctor. He diagnosed a bad case of tonsillitis; Kyoko needed some medicine and rest. Kyoko herself wasn't happy, and I thought it was hard enough being sick without being so far away from home too.

Bad things are supposed to come in threes, and it so happened that our next visitor was Al Capp, the famous cartoonist who created the popular comic strip "Li'l Abner". He was a humorist, known to be in favour of the Vietnam War, but I didn't find him in the least bit funny. How could anyone want war? Mr Capp, a conservative-looking man of about sixty, walked in declaring, "I'm that dreadful Neanderthal fascist!"

John, who could hold his own with anyone, smiled, "That's a nice introduction ... we're those famous freaks!"

Mr Capp warned the Lennons that up till now they'd been surrounded by admirers, adding, "And I may wind up to be one... You never can tell." But he wasn't there to sing John and Yoko's praises. He noted that all they seemed to be doing was lying in bed.

John answered, "We talk ten hours a day and it's functional for us to be lying down." He explained that by trying to stop war, they were doing their bit for the human race.

Al Capp didn't buy that either. He laughed, "Whatever race you're a representative of, I ain't a part of it!" and asked exactly what they thought they were doing for peace.

John reported proudly that he and Yoko had just spoken on the phone to some university students, and had successfully stopped a violent demonstration before it got out of hand. "We don't agree with violence in any form... We're telling them to protest in some other way."

I thought that was reasonable, but next Mr Capp accused John of only doing the Bed-In for money!

I could see that John was getting angry. So was I. I was ready to jump in and defend my hero – but I realized he could more than take care of himself. John told his guest in all honesty, "I could write a song in an hour and earn more money!"

The cartoonist chose not to believe that. "It won't do you any real harm," he persisted.

John shrugged, "I prefer singing to doing this, but I'm doing this for a reason."

Just to keep things even, Al Capp turned his attention to Yoko, referring to her as "Madame Nhu", who was the ruthless wife of the corrupt South Vietnamese dictator. Although this was far from a compliment, Yoko, calm as ever, didn't rise to the bait. But I was flabbergasted. What made this man think he could be offensive just because John and Yoko were famous?

Derek had also had enough. He sprang to his feet, stood between Al Capp and the Lennons and told the cartoonist furiously, "Get out … I'm not having these people insulted!"

Capp was delighted to have hit a nerve, but John softly asked his friend to calm down. "Please leave him. We asked him here."

Derek, a gentle man who hated being rude, no matter what the cause, apologized. "Forgive me."

But Al Capp wasn't as gracious as Derek. "It's not for me to forgive you, but your psychiatrist!" With that, he just walked out, laughing.

John called after him, "You just did a great deal for peace, Mr Capp. You don't know how much!"

I wanted to know what Capp was doing to make the world a better place. But John didn't seem bothered; he immediately started singing funny songs to lighten the atmosphere.

Then he had a better idea. Among the many gifts John had been showered with, he'd been given a big monster's head. He hadn't known what to do with it before – but he did now. Putting the monster on a podium, he scribbled a sign underneath: "Al Crapp". Not the greatest line John had ever written, but it certainly helped to lift our mood.

But the unpleasant incidents didn't leave a bad taste for long; everyone was having too much fun. The quiet times were the most precious, when the press and crowds were kept away, and John and Yoko would just relax with a few of us. We all got to know one another a bit better.

I didn't know it then, but at the time the Beatles were in the process of breaking up – an unthinkable thought. It would shock the world and cause tidal waves of emotion for many years; I, like millions of others, would be devastated. But during this peaceful time with John I would never have guessed what was to come.

He was a joyful man, and didn't seem to have any worries. He had just married Yoko, whom he loved deeply, and they were enjoying being together. I wasn't surprised that John was such an expert at writing love songs.

In fact, John and Yoko had recently recorded a new song, "The Ballad of John and Yoko", which had been released that week. Telling the story of how they married, it soared instantly to the top of the charts. Really, it seemed life couldn't get any better for the Lennons.

John always spoke warmly about the other Beatles, both as a band and as individuals. He was proud of everything they'd accomplished together; they were the most popular band in history, with more Number One hits than anyone. John was fulfilled both personally and professionally – and the Bed-In for Peace also seemed to be working. At that moment John was the happiest man I knew, and he liked to spread that happiness around.

John was always singing and playing his guitar; it was as if they were a part of him. He expressed himself through music, and everything was a cue for a song. All Derek had to do was mention he'd booked flights on Air Canada, and John started improvising on the spot: a song called "Good Old Air Canada" was born before my eyes.

Once when I was alone with John, he asked me what I wanted to do when I finished school. Up till then, I'd never dared admit that I wanted to be a writer. It wasn't the sort of work you could apply for down at the job centre, nor the sort of thing that most parents are glad to hear you want to do. They'd usually rather you aspire to be a doctor, a nuclear physicist or a rocket scientist.

How could I say that I'd known I wanted to be a comedy writer since I was eleven and heard my first comedy album? And that I wanted it so much that it actually hurt? I was afraid people would laugh at me – and not for the right reasons. I just couldn't imagine doing anything else. My greatest fear was that I'd have to teach, or work in an office, or heaven knows what else, for the rest of my life. I knew those were good jobs, but I would be miserable because all I wanted to do was write. I hesitated for a moment. Should I tell John? Would he understand?

I should have known better. John didn't laugh or throw cold water on my dreams. That's not what heroes do. He made my ambition seem like the most natural thing in the world. He just asked, "Have you sold anything yet?"

Excuse me? Did I hear right? The theory that someone would actually *pay* for my writing didn't compute. I'd never thought that was a possibility. Living in Montreal, I didn't even know where to begin. I explained that I'd done lots of articles for my school newspaper, and I wrote comedy sketches all the time for my friends, but I never imagined I'd be paid in real money. I didn't know that my work had a value.

John looked thoughtful for a moment, then asked if I'd heard of the *Beatles Monthly* magazine. Of course I had! The clue was in the title. It was the group's own magazine, based in Britain, and it came out once a month. It was jam-packed with the latest Beatles news, stories and photos, and I counted the days till each issue. I had them all.

John took that as a yes. He went to the phone, dialled the magazine and asked to speak to the editor. He then told him about the Bed-In, and who I was and what I was doing there. And then he added, "She's going to send you an article about me. Buy it!" After listening for a moment, he said thank you and hung up. He turned back to me and grinned. "You've just sold your first article. You're now a writer. So write!"

I asked, "Do you want to take commission?"

He laughed. How do you thank someone who's given you the greatest gift? But John didn't want to be thanked. He just wanted to give me my chance.

The Bed-In got busy again, and more famous faces kept arriving. It still seemed so unreal, I wouldn't have been surprised if Donald Duck and Mickey Mouse had shown up. They didn't – but instead we were joined by the notorious psychologist Timothy Leary. He was very alternative and believed in "exploring the mind", whatever that meant. Dr Leary was popular with hippies; it was he who coined the phrase "Turn on, tune in, drop out."

The variety of people who were drawn to the Lennons and the peace movement was incredible. I couldn't resist the chance to ask Dr Leary for his autograph; I was building up quite a collection that week.

He was gracious and wrote on my piece of paper, "You can do whatever you like in the future. You are divine!"

That sounded lovely, but I didn't really know what it meant. Dr Leary explained to me that we all have the power within us to do what we want to do; we just need the courage and confidence to find that power. He thought that you could make your own future – rather as John had told me that we could have peace if we all wanted it and worked for it. Our lives were up to us. I think I was beginning to get the message.

John and Yoko were trying to change people's thinking and make them more aware so there wouldn't be any more wars. And there was one thing John particularly wanted to do while they were in Montreal: a great ambition of his had always been to record a peace anthem. He wanted to write a song that would stand the test of time and be sung all over the world for decades to come. He decided that, with so many of his famous friends about, this was the ideal time for him to do it. I couldn't believe it. Now I might be able to watch a song actually being recorded.

As ever, once the Beatle made a decision, there was no time like the present. He sprang into action and asked me to help. John sat on the floor of the bedroom, and I perched alongside him. He explained that, with so many stars and musicians about, he wanted everyone to sing the song along with him and Yoko. He'd have

Judy Steinberg and Tommy Smothers; Rosemary
Woodruff Leary and Timothy Leary; and John,
all taking a break from the Bed-In.

to write out the lyrics. I held my breath; I had no idea what the song would be – and nor did anyone else in the world. I was getting my own sneak preview.

John was very organized and when working he concentrated deeply – the sign of a true professional, I was learning. No detail was too small. He took some of the left-over large pieces of white cardboard and the black pen he had used to draw the signs on first arriving, which now seemed like a lifetime ago. He wanted to write a cue card big enough for everyone to be able to see when they were singing. I watched as his magic words flowed out of his magic marker: "Give Peace a Chance".

John must have composed "Give Peace a Chance" sometime earlier, because he already knew the lyrics and just had to jot them down. I sat and watched as the brand-new song unfolded before my eyes; it was one of the most exciting times of my life. I'd be one of the first people ever to hear it, and I couldn't wait. This was so much cooler than racing down to the shops with my girlfriends to buy the latest Beatles album. This time, the song had come to me.

John wrote the first line across the top of the cue card. Then he started to write the verses, four of them in all, in neat columns underneath.

My favourite verse was the last, in which John listed a lot of the people who were with us in Montreal, including Tommy Smothers, Timothy Leary and Derek Taylor. As I'd got to know Derek and watched him work, I felt he was one of the hitherto unsung stars of the Bed-In. I knew that none of this could have taken place without him. Derek managed to turn chaos into order, and did it calmly and kindly too. He was definitely one in a million and I was glad he was being acknowledged.

I was also thrilled to see Tommy Cooper mentioned; he was one of my favourite English comedians and could make me ache with laughter every time he performed. I knew by now that John and I shared a similar sense of humour, which may have been what drew me to him in the first place. I was positive that all these people would get a kick out of being immortalized in a Lennon song.

As I struggled to see over his shoulder, John wrote the chorus line of his new song across the bottom of the cue card, and I knew I was looking at a hit.

He finished writing the cue card, then studied it for a moment. Yet he still wasn't satisfied with the actual card. He'd written on only one half of it, and now felt that it wouldn't be big enough for everyone to see. So he gave me a second piece of cardboard, handed me his magic marker and asked me to write the song out again, only this time making it twice as large.

In the meantime, John turned his thoughts to re-

cording the music. Of course he himself would be playing guitar, and he asked Tommy Smothers to play on
the song as well. Tommy was eager to join him – who
wouldn't have been? – but he didn't have his guitar with
him. He said he could only play a Gibson, so John lent
him one, then performed the song for him, showing
him and saying, "It's in the key of C."

Tommy wanted to put in some of his own bits, but
John – who was, after all, used to being the leader of
the world's most successful band – said no. They didn't
have time to try new things out anyway. He made
Tommy go back to the beginning of the song and play
it over and over again, till he was happy with every last
detail. John had obviously got to be a rock star not only
thanks to talent but also through hard work and per-
severance. Since there were only two guitars, John decided it would sound best if he and Tommy doubled up
on the parts, and they played together in unison till he
was satisfied.

As I copied the lyrics, and listened to them play, I
no longer envied the girls in the studio audience of *The
Ed Sullivan Show*. Unlike those other fans, I was getting
my own personal concert. I hung on every note.

I finished the cue card and cringed as I saw how
in places my writing had sloped off a bit to the left or
right. But luckily, John approved it. I felt proud that
my card was going to be used for his recording. I asked

John what he wanted me to do with the one he had written – and he said, "You can have it!"

This had to be the souvenir of the century! I was overwhelmed and asked John if he was sure.

As ever, he knew his own mind. "Keep it," he insisted. "It'll be worth something one day."

I wasn't going to argue. I told him it would take pride of place in my bedroom. I couldn't wait to show it to my friends. "This is the best swap in the history of swaps. My cue card for yours – what a deal!"

Then it was time to concentrate on the actual recording. John decided that he wanted some tambourines in the background. But it was nine-thirty in the evening and all the music shops would be shut. Wherever would we find a tambourine? I had learned this week never to say never; where there's a will, there's a tambourine. I had a brainwave and remembered our Hare Krishna friends, with their drums, flutes and tambourines. They'd be perfect. It took only one call. As ever, they were very obliging – they headed straight over. John was beginning to get his band together.

While all this was going on, Derek was arranging the technical side. John had asked for some eight-track recording equipment. Derek rang Andre Perry, a young record producer, who had a studio not too far away in a suburb of Montreal. He came as fast as he could, eager to help record the song.

Andre and Derek supervised as the bulky equipment was brought into the room. Microphones and tape recorders were put into place, and Andre ran sound checks. Since this wasn't a proper studio, he needed to put screens around the room, which was quite large, to contain the music so the recording would sound professional.

John and Yoko also wanted to capture this historic session on film, so movie cameras were brought in too. A film director set up lights and tried to find the best angles for his camera. I watched in awe as everything happened around me.

When it was all ready, John called his guests back in and organized his band. Everyone was excited beyond belief to be there. No one had expected to be making a record with John and Yoko – least of all me.

As well as Tommy Smothers, Petula Clark, Dick Gregory and Timothy Leary, more people arrived: the beat poet Alan Ginsberg, Murray the K – a New York DJ – and many others. Derek joined in, as did George Urquhart, the bodyguard. John decided to christen this unique group the Plastic Ono Band. Everyone was ready to rock. The excitement grew as John started rehearsing the song. People quickly picked it up – it was a catchy number! At about midnight, John was satisfied and gave the order for the song to be recorded, right there and then. This was it.

As I heard the music start, I felt a tingle run through me. It was incredible hearing John play his guitar, singing and throwing his soul into it. I grabbed a tambourine and started bashing away; it was my finest hour. George clapped his hands and Derek Taylor sang along loudly too. The greatest jam session of all time had begun.

Everyone started singing from the cue card I had written – and I was pleased to see that no one stumbled over my handwriting. The sound the Plastic Ono Band produced together was electrifying. It seemed there was happiness and magic all around; the music made us float on air. I was momentarily overwhelmed by all the emotion. For that moment, in room 1742 of the Queen Elizabeth Hotel in Montreal, I believed it was possible for us to change the world. Everyone should have that feeling all the time.

The sound swelled. I saw Yoko singing with all her heart. Timothy Leary was knocking some rhythm sticks together in time to the music. Everybody clapped to the beat, or pounded on the doors, or made their own do-it-yourself drum kits out of tables. Our group sang as loudly as we could. The film cameras whirred; the stills cameras flashed all around. It was the party of all parties and the greatest show on Earth, and I had a front-row seat.

I was shocked to remind myself that I was actually there, in the middle, being a part of it. I was there with John Lennon and Yoko Ono, making history. I wasn't reading about this in some fan magazine, or watching it on a television show, or hearing about it on the radio. It was me, Gail, actually recording a song with John Lennon and all these stars. I was aware I should savour every second. Nothing like it had ever happened to me before or ever would again. I knew it was the event of a lifetime.

We all kept chanting John's chorus, truly wanting everyone to give love and peace a chance. We meant it, and we believed that what we were doing could and would make a difference. We were convinced that the world would heed John's wise words. This was a protest, but with a difference: it was a peaceful one.

I didn't want the song or the feeling to end – none of us did – but of course it had to. At last John brought the number to a close. The moment it was over, everyone cheered, clapped and hugged one another tightly. We knew we had just done something special. We all looked over to John to see his reaction. He shouted out, "OK! Lights out! Let's rest!"

We all laughed, but I could see John was pleased. He had done what he'd set out to do. He had written a peace anthem that would stand the test of time.

As John said, you should have been there.

FIVE

GET BACK

The next morning I stumbled in, bleary-eyed to say the least. It wasn't just the previous night's recording session, which I'd replayed over and over in my mind till the wee hours like a favourite tape. Each night when I got home, I'd write up my diary of the day's events, sometimes till quite late. Every moment was so precious that I didn't want to forget a thing.

Counting the days I'd been at the Bed-In, I suddenly realized, to my horror, that it would soon be over. Of course I knew it had only ever been supposed to be for eight days and that was never going to be enough. I couldn't bear the thought of it ending – but on the other hand I knew I'd have lots of time to think about it afterwards. So I decided, why start grieving now?

Already I knew how much I was going to miss the Lennons. I just vowed to enjoy every minute.

When I got to the suite, I asked Derek when they'd be leaving. I had heard that they'd be going to Ottawa next, for a peace rally at the university. Derek looked surprised and gently pulled me to one side. "Shh! Not in front of the press – it's supposed to be a secret!"

I told him I'd just heard it on the television news, and he sighed. It was getting harder and harder to contain everything that was happening all around. The Bed-In had a life all of its own.

During a break, Derek gave me some money and asked me to buy an extra suitcase from the shop in the lobby. The Lennons had been given so many gifts, they'd definitely need another case. As I was leaving the room, I heard a strange noise coming from somewhere in the hotel. It was an echo of feet, and shouts, getting louder and louder. I didn't know what it was, but I didn't like it. It sounded almost like a stampede, like the ones you hear in Westerns. Instinctively I shut the door and hurried back inside.

I found Derek on the phone to a policeman, who had just called the suite. Derek went pale as he listened. This didn't look good. The policeman told Derek that a group of about two hundred young people had just stormed the barriers downstairs and were making their way up to room 1742. The police didn't have enough manpower to hold them back.

The mob had marched from a local park on the mountain, where they were holding some sort of demonstration. When they got to the hotel, there were so many of them that they managed to crash through the barricades. They were now climbing all the way up to the seventeenth floor to see John and Yoko. As the police tried to handle the situation, all of us inside were advised to stay put.

I could hear the crowd getting nearer, and I was scared. Who wouldn't be? I'd never dealt with a mob before. It's not the kind of thing you learn at school. I saw John coming up behind me with Kyoko, who was holding his hand, and I relaxed for a moment. If John was there, I reassured myself, everything would be all right. But to my amazement he was panic-stricken: "Mobs are the only things I'm petrified of!"

I hadn't thought John was afraid of anything, but I could see he meant it. I was aware that the Beatles had been mobbed many times in their career. John must have been only too familiar with the serious damage that hundreds of marauding people could do, to both property and people, even if they didn't mean to. He was right to be alarmed. As the mob made their way up to our floor, we could hear their footsteps pounding and their shouts advancing. I had a sick feeling in the pit of my stomach.

John suddenly looked round for Kyoko – but she wasn't there. We realized that as we'd turned away for a second to talk, she had opened the door, curious to see what all the excitement was about – and now, before we could stop her, she dashed out into the corridor. Horrified, we saw her race towards the noise.

Faster even than John, I raced out and got to Kyoko first. I snatched her up, holding her tightly as I tried to turn back. The next moment, I felt John putting his arms round us both. He pulled us both back inside the suite, calling, "Come on!"

He yanked us into a bedroom where Yoko, Derek, Tommy Smothers and the others had all taken shelter. Kyoko ran to her mother for protection. John yelled at us to lock all the doors, which we quickly did. He said we should stand in front of the doors and push against them, in case the fans tried to break them down. I didn't like the sound of that but I obeyed, my heart thumping. Only seconds later, the mob broke down the door to the outer suite and we heard them cascading in. We held our breath. They were now much too close for comfort, but there was nothing we could do. We felt completely helpless.

Worst of all, we didn't know who these people were or what they wanted. Were they friends, foes or fans? Might they be terrorists?

There's a basic problem with mobs: even if individually every single person is wonderful and well-meaning, together they might still cause a lot of harm. This mob was capable of hurting us whether they meant to or not. Together, they were dangerous, because they were out of control and excited.

Matters quickly went from bad to worse when the crowd started beating on the door, which anyway didn't look terribly strong to me. It began to shake, and so did I. That flimsy door was all that stood between us and them; I didn't think it would hold up for long. My mind began to race. What would happen if they broke through? Would we be crushed? Might we be trampled to death?

Kyoko clung even tighter to Yoko. Through the noise, we could hear the mob calling for John. Derek put his foot down: he wasn't prepared to risk John going out to meet them. There was no way the Beatle could just step out into the throng and hope for the best. But Derek also knew that John was going to have to do something quickly before this turned into a tragedy.

John told the police to quieten the group so he could speak. Then, shouting so he could be heard by the fans, he told them,"I don't want anyone to get hurt. We're all here for love and peace, and I know you don't mean to do anyone any harm. But you're frightening a lot of people, including a little girl."

John wouldn't leave the room, but instead asked for

a spokesman to be chosen by the group to come in and see him. He would speak to that one person only, and give him or her a message which would be passed on to the rest. We felt relieved when they finally agreed.

We were surprised when the door opened a crack, and a young hippie girl squeezed inside. It was funny, because when she was alone she wasn't scary at all; she was just like everyone else. She explained that the group had been demonstrating for peace on the mountain, and just wanted to see John and Yoko.

John spoke to her honestly. This uncontrolled frenzy wasn't helping the peace process at all. Quite the contrary, it was damaging it. "You're only giving the Establishment more reason to attack."

The girl felt ashamed. She knew John was right.

He advised her, "Go back to the mountain and demonstrate peacefully."

John asked everyone to go back downstairs and promised that if they did, he'd broadcast a special radio message, just for them. He asked everyone to trust him, just as he had always trusted them.

The girl apologized, saying, "We never meant to hurt you or your friends." She looked around. "I feel so sorry for you, crowded into this room."

I thought that was an understatement. It was a frightening glimpse of how John and Yoko – and many other celebrities – were sometimes forced to live.

Meanwhile John was gathering armfuls of the white flowers that were all around the room; he gave them to the girl, asking that they be shared with the others as a gift from him. She assured him they would be. John thanked her and the girl left.

We all breathed a huge sigh of relief as we heard the crowd disperse and the noises outside quickly became distant murmurs. Suddenly all was quiet. The danger was over … for now. But I wondered if there would be a next time?

Derek arranged for the radio broadcast to the fans that John had promised. The Lennons wanted to speak to everyone and discourage them from ever doing this kind of thing again.

On air, John spoke about "the meaning of peace, in every part of your life. It doesn't cover only wars, but our everyday dealings with the people around us too." I really took what he said to heart, and I knew that the hippies from the mountain would understand too. Just as he and Yoko were finishing their broadcast, Kyoko squeezed in between them and joined them at the microphone. She wanted to speak. She spoke into the microphone like a pro, pleading sweetly, "Will you all do something for me? Please stop fighting and have Peace, just for me?" We were all amazed. Obviously Kyoko had learned some important lessons during the Bed-In. We just hoped that everyone else had too.

. J spoke to the ring leader, a 15 year old
girl. He told her to tell, the others to go back to the
mountain. He said that they were only giving the establishment more reason to attack. J gave the leader loads
of flowers to give to the mob. They dispersed. Jand Y
went on radio to speak to all. K went to the mike, and
said in her sweetest voice, "Will you all do something
for me? Please stop fighting and have Peace, just for
me?" We were all surprised

But it wasn't long before John and Yoko were called
upon to be peacemakers once again. Just a few hours
later, over thirty thousand people in Berkeley, California, marched through the city to protest in the People's Park – till recently, a derelict site owned by the
University of California. Wanting this neglected spot
to be used for the enjoyment of the entire community,
one thousand people had helped turn it into a beautiful park. Now developers wanted to build on it. Students staged a protest, while a small aeroplane flew over
the city trailing a banner that read "LET A THOUSAND
PARKS BLOOM". The authorities decided to crack down
and sent in 250 police officers to stop them. Feelings on
both sides were running high. In that situation, with the
two sides confronting each other, things could go badly
wrong.

It did, when the National Guard, a military organization, arrived with their guns and bayonets. The police
lobbed tear-gas canisters into the crowd, causing injury

and panic. The situation was getting dangerous.

The peace protesters were ready for action. Once again, the Lennons took to the airwaves and counselled the Berkeley marchers to avoid violence at all costs. John advised, "Don't kill yourselves... No bit of grass is worth that! No park is worth dying for!" He begged them not to use violence, and to retreat. He could only hope people would listen.

After that broadcast was finished, we all slumped into chairs. It had been quite a day; we were all mentally and physically exhausted. I could see that campaigning for peace was a full-time business, and one that took a lot of guts to pursue. I admired John and Yoko, who had genuine concerns for peace and for the future of the world. They were rich, famous people who could have done nothing but have fun and enjoy the fruits of their success. Instead, they were using their talents, resources and energies to try to make the world a better place – sometimes at considerable cost to themselves. Once while we were talking quietly, John confided to me, "My biggest fear is that, one day, a nutter with a gun is going to get me." A chill went through me and I felt as though someone had walked on my grave. It was such a horrendous idea, I didn't even want to think about it.

In one quiet moment, Derek took me aside for a chat. He told me that he and the Lennons would be moving on, taking their peace campaign to Ottawa and Toronto next – and they all wanted to know if I would like to join them.

I'd never been so flabbergasted since the last time I was flabbergasted (it seemed to be happening a lot these days). I'd been trying hard not to feel upset about the thought of the Bed-In finishing; I didn't know how I was going to find a way to say goodbye to all my new friends. Now it seemed I might not have to. I had absolutely no idea what to say.

Derek explained that I could carry on doing what I'd been doing for the past week, giving a hand wherever necessary. I would enjoy travelling with the group, staying in the best hotels with them and seeing new places. Yoko also had said it would be lovely if I could come, because I'd built up such a good relationship with Kyoko – whom I adored.

Derek hinted that if things worked out after Ottawa and Toronto, and everyone was happy, maybe I could join the entourage full-time. That shocked me even more; I had never thought of making a career out of this. He looked to me for an answer. What did I think?

I knew that my holidays were coming. It wouldn't be as if I'd be missing any school – although of course to me that would have made the offer even more attractive. And I'd never felt so flattered; I couldn't believe they all wanted me to become part of their group. This seemed such a huge step. And anyway, even if I wanted to go, would my parents let me?

Thoughtfully, Derek offered to ring my mother. Over the past week I had told each of them so much about the other that they chatted like old friends. Derek assured Mum that everyone promised to look after me well. By now, my mother trusted Derek and the Lennons. She had seen me come to no harm; quite the contrary, in fact – she'd seen me take on responsibility and have the time of my life. She discussed it with my father.

After what seemed an eternity, Derek handed me the phone. I was waiting for some kind of verdict to be pronounced from on high when Mum, to my everlasting surprise, said something I'd never expected in a million years. She said it was my choice.

I thought I hadn't heard right. Could this really be my parents?

This was something new; until then, I'd always been told what to do by everyone in my life. At home, the rules were clear. I knew when I was supposed to get up, go to bed, eat, study, walk the dog and clean my room. At school, there were yet more rules. I was told what I was expected to wear, study, write and even think.

Now I felt as if I was being released into the wild … the choice was going to be mine. I was excited, but also scared. I realized this was the first really big decision I'd ever had to make.

I saw that Derek was still looking at me curiously, waiting for my reply. I told him honestly, "I don't know!"

He laughed – but I swore it wasn't that I was playing hard to get. There was so much to think about, so many people to talk to and plans to work out. The whole idea was overwhelming, although in a happy way.

Derek told me to take my time, but that they'd have to know tomorrow, before they left. I said I would sleep on it.

Naturally I didn't sleep a wink that night.

SIX

HELLO, GOODBYE

I arrived at the hotel early the next morning because I had a lot to do. Outside room 1742, George and I greeted each other sadly. I had grown fond of him over the past eight days, and I knew I would miss him. I was sure life would become a lot quieter for him now – maybe too quiet. He told me that in his long career he'd taken care of kings, queens, stars and other VIPs, but this time had been the most memorable.

George had already said his goodbyes to the Lennons. John had called him over to thank him for the great week. He also wanted to know what George thought of "Give Peace a Chance". John was eager for his first review – I guess stars are as insecure as the rest of us.

George told him that he'd served with the Canadian

Army in Korea, so he fully backed John and Yoko's peace message. Touched, John gave him a *Yellow Submarine* album which he and Yoko had signed specially for him.

Just before I went in, George confided to me, "You'll never realize how closely you were watched with Kyoko that first day. Everyone was afraid of a kidnapping plot." I was glad I'd passed the audition. But I was also reminded of yet another aspect of celebrity life.

Inside the suite, John and Yoko were getting ready to go. I was taken aback to see them wearing their casual street clothes. John was wearing his white linen suit again, only this time with a smart black shirt and colourful tie. He looked oddly respectable. Yoko was in her white trouser suit. I couldn't help saying, "My, you scrub up well!" I'd seen them only in white silk pyjamas or white nighties for the last eight days; funny how you get used to things. But now they were ready to re-enter the world.

Derek greeted me and asked where my bag was. I took him to one side. Even I couldn't believe what I was saying as I stammered, "I've never been so flattered in all my life. And thank you – but I'm not going to come." Derek listened intently as I went on. "Don't get me wrong, I've thought about nothing else all night. And I've loved every second and everyone. But I don't think it's right for me."

Derek nodded as I tried not to cry. I could scarcely believe I was giving up this golden opportunity to spend more time with my heroes, to travel and to go on meeting famous people. If I chose, I could still be with them as they lived their exciting lives. But there was the problem: I wanted to live *my own* exciting life.

It had taken all this to make me realize that I wanted to go to university and study English, which I loved. Most of all, I wanted to be a writer and to be involved in comedy. I knew all that would be impossible if I were travelling here, there and everywhere with the Lennons. After a while, every hotel and city, no matter how luxurious, would begin to look the same. Four walls are four walls, no matter what country you're in.

I didn't want to be transported from hotel to hotel in limos with blacked-out windows, surrounded by police and bodyguards. The previous night I'd had nightmares about the mob storming the suite, and I'd always be anxious about something like that happening again, as it very likely would. And next time we might not be so lucky.

I'd witnessed at first hand some of the downsides of how celebrities live. I'd seen how John and Yoko could never go out on the spur of the moment, even for a walk in a park on a sunny day. They couldn't just pop into a shop, or go to a film or visit a friend. And it would be hard for anyone who travelled with them, too, because understandably they craved company. Nobody wants to be alone in strange hotel rooms.

It dawned on me that's why celebrities have entourages. Just about all of them are surrounded by people: their employees, friends – or both, like Derek. They become the star's substitute family and often stay with them for years. I guess if stars can't get out into the world, then they have to bring the world to them. But that can be suffocating at times too.

It was an honour to be asked to join them, one that I would always treasure. But this taste of the rock-star experience had been just enough. The past eight days had been an unbelievable adventure, but I couldn't see myself living that way for weeks, months or possibly years. Stars often have to live their lives like that, but I didn't. I wanted to begin my own world.

I think Derek, both a writer himself and incredibly kind, understood. He asked, "In that case, would you accept a gift from John? I'm sure he'd like to give you some money."

I surprised even myself but I shook my head. "Thanks, but I couldn't accept money. I did it all for John and Yoko, and because I believe in peace. And I was rewarded enough by meeting amazing people like you and Tommy Smothers and Petula Clark!"

Derek insisted I take some money for all my hard work. "Students can always find a use for it." I couldn't argue with him there. He also gave me a kiss and a copy of *Yellow Submarine* which John had been playing all week. Derek told me to contact him if I came to London. I assured him he could bet on that!

I took Kyoko out for a last ice-cream to say goodbye. I didn't make a big deal out of it because I didn't want to make her feel sad; I could see she was excited about moving on and that was good. I'd grown very close to that beautiful child and I wished her only happiness. After finishing our treat, we went back upstairs to find the Lennons.

John was in the bedroom, packing. I thanked him for his incredible offer but told him that regretfully I wouldn't be coming with them. He nodded, thought for a moment, then asked, "Do you have an autographed photo of me?"

This was so unexpected that I laughed and the words were out of my mouth before I realized: "Why? Are times so hard that you have to give them away?"

John grinned and reminded me that I hadn't got the autograph I'd asked him for on the first day. He rummaged round and found an 8-inch x 10-inch glossy black-and-white photo of him and Yoko lying in bed, entwined. He fetched Yoko and they signed it together: "To Gail. Thank you!! Peace and love. Yoko Ono and John Lennon".

Yoko said she couldn't thank me enough and asked

for my address so she'd know where to reach me. Then she went to help Kyoko get ready, and I was left alone with John. I was going to find it hard to say goodbye, almost impossible. I didn't know if I would ever see him again – but I didn't dare let myself think about that.

I started to help John with his packing. Sadly I stowed his guitar in its case. Looking into his warm brown eyes, I asked how I could ever thank him for everything he'd done for me.

John and Yoko had let me participate in their Bed-In; it was the first time I had ever felt useful and needed. I'd had time to get to know them and lots of other extraordinary people. John had also made me a gift of his handwritten lyrics of "Give Peace a Chance", which were already propped up on my bedroom dresser at home, waiting to be framed.

Most of all, John had believed in me and given me confidence to believe that I could be a writer or anything else I wanted to be. Now that I'd sold my first article, I couldn't wait to start writing more. I knew I was going to be OK. Both John and my parents had taught me an important lesson this week: it was all up to me. From now on, life was going to be what I made it. I was grateful for that.

John smiled at me. "You're beautiful."

No one had ever said that to me before. It felt wonderful. He said he would see me again – and I wanted

to believe that. But this was different from all the other times; I knew I wouldn't be coming back to the hotel the next day, saying good morning to George and sailing into the suite. How would I ever get close to the Lennons again, once they'd moved on? Lightning doesn't strike twice, and I'd be greedy to hope for it.

Noticing I looked glum, John took something out of his bag and handed it to me. It was a card with an address and phone number on it. He explained, "No matter where in the world I am, if you want me, they'll always know how to get hold of me."

I was stunned, but even this didn't reassure me. I was positive no one would help a kid who just rang up and asked to speak to John. I shrugged and asked, "What do I tell them?"

John looked at me in surprise and said simply, "The truth. You tell them you're my friend."

That was the greatest gift of all. I tucked the card into my handbag. To me, it instantly became a magic number and I swore I would always keep it safe.

John added, "If you ever need anything, I'll always take care of you."

My address book, in which I recorded John and Yoko's contact details.

I decided to go before I broke down and embarrassed us both. Worse, John might take his card back. As I said goodbye, John put his arms around me and gave me a big hug and a kiss. I can still remember his embrace. He was incredibly slim; I was surprised at how bony he felt. He'd obviously not been getting enough to eat at the Bed-In. Also his beard felt tickly – but a great sort of tickly.

We smiled as I left and headed for the lift, happy. This was certainly easier than scampering up the fire escape and climbing in through a window, as I'd done on my way in. Eight days is a very long time.

Thank you, John and Yoko. You gave peace and me a chance.

John and Yoko's Christmas message
from 1969. It's still apt.

WAR IS OVER!

IF YOU WANT IT

Happy Christmas from John & Yoko

AFTERWORD

STRAWBERRY FIELDS FOREVER

There was life after the Bed-In, but it wasn't always as exciting. To everyone's heartache, the Beatles broke up in 1970, although they continued to be superstars individually. John and Yoko moved to New York City, which isn't far away from Montreal. But as it happened, after university I moved to London, where I became a writer.

John had achieved his ambition to write a peace anthem that would stand the test of time. "Give Peace a Chance" was sung by half a million demonstrators in Washington, DC, during a peace rally later in 1969, and it's still sung today.

And yes, I did see John again.

As he'd promised, his magic number worked. I

didn't ring it every day, of course, but I used it a few times and John always seemed happy to hear from me. I also kept up with him through mutual friends and, even easier, of course, the newspapers.

I took it for granted that there would always be time for us to see each other again. But on 8 December 1980, as the Lennons entered the Dakota apartment building where they lived, John was shot by Mark David Chapman. John died almost instantly.

"My biggest fear is that, one day, a nutter with a gun is going to get me." His words came back to me. His greatest nightmare had come true. The shock waves ricocheted around the world. Like so many others, I mourned him and miss him to this day.

The cue card with his handwritten lyrics to "Give Peace a Chance" had moved with me to London. It hung on the wall of my study, a souvenir of happy times. Over the years, I'd often wondered why I'd been given those lyrics. Perhaps now I knew: to get John and Yoko's peace message out to the world once again. I hope I've used them to honour John's memory.

Thanks again, John and Yoko. May your words continue to be heard for ever. Love and peace.

ACKNOWLEDGEMENTS

Many thanks to Gill Evans, who thought there might be a book in my story – and, thank goodness, was right. I also want to thank my friend and agent Mike Sharland, for his help and encouragement and for keeping me sane throughout. A special wave to George Urquhart, the former Director of Security at the Queen Elizabeth Hotel, and John and Yoko's bodyguard at the Bed-In; invaluable both then and now.

And a big scream-out to John, Paul, George and Ringo, because it all started with them. I'm still a Beatlemaniac forty years on … even though my parents said I'd grow out of it!

INTERNET LINKS

Here are John's original lyrics to "Give Peace a Chance". My mother thought they were cluttering up my bedroom and wanted to throw them out. Luckily I didn't let her!
http://blog.nj.com/ledgerupdates_impact/2008/05/ large_lyrics.jpg

The best thing about auctioning the "Give Peace a Chance" lyrics was hearing the song played all around the world again, along with the Lennons' peace message. I like to think that may have been why John gave me the lyrics. CBS filmed this short piece about it:
http://www.youtube.com/watch?v=L_p-jp45W4A

You can see me briefly in this clip, standing behind Al Capp with the photographers, and you can also hear me laugh out loud a lot!

http://www.youtube.com/watch?v=iYxFO8o-t2E

Alder Hey Children's Hospital IMAGINE Appeal

This famous children's hospital is based in John's home town of Liverpool and cares for around 250,000 sick children each year. Donations to IMAGINE go towards medical research, buying vital equipment and improving sick children's lives worldwide.

IMAGINE has the support of Yoko Ono, who has allowed one of John's sketches to be used as its logo so, once again, his drawings are helping people.

http://www.imagineappeal.com/

WHY

WhyHunger is a not-for-profit registered organization which fights hunger and poverty in the United States and around the world, by supporting communities and building self-reliance. It teaches people how to empower themselves and is also supported by Yoko Ono.

http://www.whyhunger.org/

GAIL RENARD

Gail is an award-winning screenwriter and performer. After the Bed-In and graduating from university, she arrived in London, where she started writing television scripts. Gail won a prestigious British Academy of Film and Television Arts (BAFTA) award for the BBC TV teenage comedy/drama series she created, *Custer's Last Stand-Up*. Her many series include the C4 comedy *Get Up, Stand Up*, the *Famous Five* film series and BBC TV's *Chucklevision*. Gail writes books for both children and adults, and is currently co-writing a film and stage comedy.

As a performer Gail has appeared in many TV and radio shows, and she has featured for many years as both presenter and judge of one of ITV's major shows,

The British Comedy Awards.

Gail is a former Chair of the Writers' Guild of Great Britain, and its current TV Chair. She has never stopped fighting for people's rights – a lesson she learned from John and Yoko.

Here's me with the original SGT. PEPPER drum-skin, designed by artist Peter Blake. And the beat goes on!

Opposite and overleaf: A dress I wore at the Bed-In (but don't any more!) and the "Give Peace A Chance" lyrics in John's own handwriting.

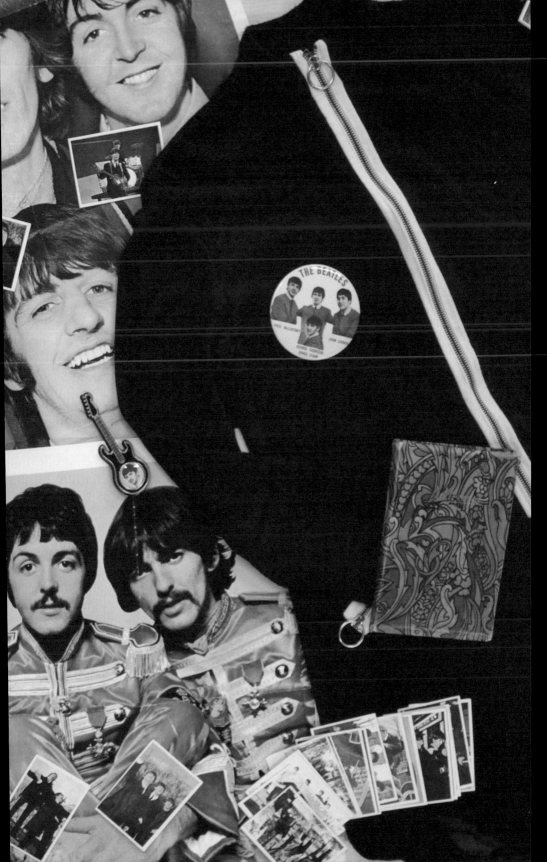

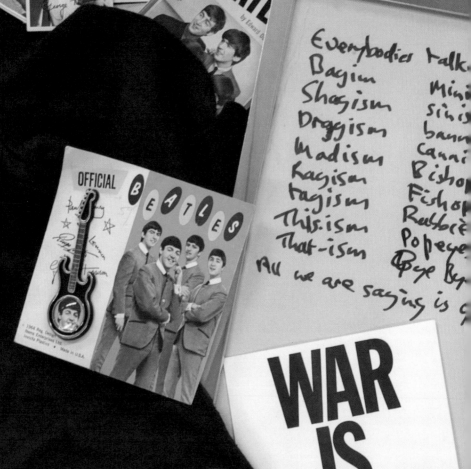